ETERNAL WISDOM

The Esoteric Gnosis of Perennial Philosophy

GWENDOLYN TAUNTON

Eternal Wisdom: The Esoteric Gnosis of Perennial Philosophy
Gwendolyn Taunton

Thema Classification:
QRAB (Philosophy of Religion), VXW (Mysticism), QRVK2 (Mysticism), QRYC (Esoteric Religions).
978-0-6487660-5-6
MANTICORE PRESS
www.manticore.press

We are living in what the Greeks called the right time for a "metamorphosis of the gods," i.e., of the fundamental principles and symbols. This peculiarity of our time, which is certainly not of our conscious choosing, is the expression of the unconscious man within us who is changing. Coming generations will have to take account of this momentous transformation if humanity is not to destroy itself through the might of its own technology and science.

Carl Gustav Jung

CONTENTS

INTRODUCTION

A decade has now passed since the original publication of this work, which was in *Primordial Traditions*, initially a free online publication. Since then much has changed. *Primordial Traditions*, despite having begun as a simple homemade PDF, rapidly progressed in popularity. Before long *Primordial Traditions* was issued in book form and won a prestigious literary award in New Zealand – the *Ashton Wylie Award for Literary Excellence*, which was presented by the Mayor of Auckland and the Society of Authors. The $10,000 award money was then used to establish an independent publishing company. Following my decision to leave New Zealand due to a series of destructive earthquakes, this business was then relocated to Australia.

This new revised edition consists purely of my own work. It has also been revised in accordance with my evolving perception on spiritual traditions. As a consequence of this, the new version has also been renamed *Eternal Wisdom: The Esoteric Gnosis of Perennial Philosophy*, which is a more accurate description of its content and difficult to misconstrue. This rebranding provides a clear demarcation between the quasi-political cults espousing 'Traditionalism' and perennial philosophy. Whilst Traditionalism was once a purely spiritual and intellectual practice, it has since been tainted by the presence of politically subversive elements, and unless one is active in that milieu, it should no longer be used. As I am not a political Traditionalist, I will not be using this nomenclature.

The terms *perennial philosophy* and *Primordial Tradition* are associated with authors such as René Guénon, Frithjof Schuon, Ananda Coomaraswamy, Nicolás Gómez Dávila, Huston Smith, and Aldous Huxley. The term by which it was first known to Europe, *perenni philosophia,* was originally used by Agostino Steuco in *De perenni philosophia libri x* (1540). This then evolved to become the *prisca theologia,* later known as the *religio perennis* or *philosophia perennis* (perennial philosophy). The most recent work on perennial philosophy is found in the work of Huston Smith. It is Smith who first advocated the use of the term *Primordial Tradition* as a substitute for *Traditionalism.*

According to anthropology, human consciousness dawned when art and religion were created, and thus these two concepts are inextricably entwined. The first use of art was in ritual, and the initial use of symbols was for religious purposes. Taking this as *a priori*, the purest manifestation of the Primordial Tradition is, therefore, one which communicates directly in a language of symbols, which is akin to Plato's theory of forms. Although Plato was the first to draw upon the idea that symbols may adopt an independent 'reality,' he was by no means the last. Carl Jung, a pioneer in the field of psychology, adopted a similar notion in his theory of archetypes. Developing out of Jung's work, the field of archetypal psychology took this concept even further, explaining myth as interpretations of many different psychological processes.

Through emerging academic disciplines such as the History of Religions and Comparative Mythology, the scope of perennial philosophy once more expanded: religious ideas could be interpreted and understood in terms of their relationship with one another. Perennial philosophy is independent and not part of any single spiritual tradition, and yet it is inherent in every doctrine and ritual. Its presence can be found in all things that employ the use of symbolism as a form of language and which rely on abstract cognition as a mode of expression to communicate with the numinous.

The Primordial Tradition, therefore, does not represent any particular spiritual tradition or path in its own right, but rather is concerned with the language and medium by which culture, religion, and ritual are interpreted. As such, it is truly neutral, and it is therefore possible for those studying the Primordial Tradition to belong to any spiritual tradition. Across all cultures, the transmission of the Primordial Tradition remains constant, whether it is within the Hindu, Christian, Heathen, Shamanic, or any other religion. Polytheist, henotheist, or monotheist: the dialectic, the *nous,* and the *logos* of divinity remains the same. The source does not fluctuate.

Gwendolyn Taunton

Winter Solstice, 2020

PHILOSOPHIA PERENNIS

PERENNIAL PHILOSOPHY REBRANDED

Jung, Smith, & The Primordial Tradition

Remember that I have remembered / and pass on the tradition.
Ezra Pound, *Cantos*

The Primordial Tradition is an obscure and widely misunderstood term, and although used repeatedly in the works of René Guénon and Frithjof Schuon, it remains largely undefined. The most precise description of the Primordial Tradition is provided by a more recent author, Huston Smith, a professor of comparative religion. Smith was the first to utilize the Primordial Tradition as a substitute term for perennial philosophy. Smith attempts to justify his replacement of the term in the introduction to his popular book, *Forgotten Truth: The Primordial Tradition*:

> The reader will recognize the affinity of this thesis with what has been called "the perennial philosophy." I am not unhappy with that phrase, but to bring out the fact

that this particular philosophy nowhere originated, nor has it succeeded in maintaining itself operatively, save in a cultic context – a context that works to transform lives as well as minds – I prefer the less exclusively intellectual designation "the primordial tradition" (primordial: existing from the beginning; fundamental.)[1]

Smith's motivation in adopting this premise is easy to comprehend; from its current standpoint of existing purely in a philosophical context, perennial philosophy sets itself apart from mundane daily existence, manifesting as a strictly intellectual phenomenon which is beyond the grasp of the average reader. The term 'Primordial Tradition' provides this school of thought with a worldly and tangible presence, which is no longer restricted to the dusty cloisters of university libraries. Tradition, as espoused by Huston Smith, becomes accessible to the mainstream. However, if we were to ask the common man on the street if he could explain to us what perennial philosophy is, one would most likely receive a garrulous "no," accompanied by a blank stare. Perennial philosophy has simply been so over-intellectualized that it has become confined to the realm of 'ivory tower academic idealism,' which no longer has any relevance to the outside world. For this philosophy to survive, one must, to a certain extent, mute the philosophers. This does not to deny the rich intellectual heritage of philosophy, however.

To discover the meaning of the Primordial Tradition, one must first explain the meaning of perennial philosophy. The term 'perennial philosophy' (*philosophia perennis*) was utilized by Gottfried Leibniz to describe

---

[1]   SMITH, H., *Forgotten Truth: The Primordial Tradition* (New York: Harper & Row, 1976), x.

the eternal philosophy that underlies all religions, and in particular, their mystical or esoteric components – in this way it is similar to the Hindu idea of *Sanatana Dharma*. As such, the *philosophia perennis* is an intellectual transmission of gnosis, based on the study of religions not in isolation from each other, but rather in conjunction, where the underlying ideas converge, independent of the concept of *communitas* (defined by Victor Turner as the exoteric or social aspect of religion). Because of the cultural boundaries erected by collective group identities, "religions are cut off from one another by barriers of mutual incomprehension."[2]

The same ties of collective behavior that serve to bind a community together as a distinct cultural group can also hinder the process of understanding different spiritual traditions. Schuon elaborates on the nature of this barrier by stating that, "There is no metaphysical or spiritual difference between a truth manifested by temporal facts and a truth expressed by other symbols, under a mythological form for example; the modes of manifestation correspond to the mental requirements of the different groups of humanity."[3] This idea expresses the notion that the symbols found in spiritual traditions possess ontological values. However, the original meaning of a symbol or metaphor can be distorted by the communal aspect of exoteric religion, as it is more susceptible to being influenced by outside factors stemming from other aspects of a culture, especially its political components. As esoteric religion is less dependent on social interactions, it naturally possesses a certain amount of immunity to cultural paradigm shifts and political whims, although

---

[2] SCHUON, F., *Gnosis: Divine Wisdom* (Middlesex: Perennial Books, 1990), 11.

[3] Ibid., 18.

it is dependent on the exoteric to be transmitted. Thus, external factors can change the interpretation of a symbol, and eventually, erode the tradition itself.

Furthermore, distortions can also occur in the mode of transmission itself, via mistranslation, misrepresentation, or miscomprehension. These errors in communication do not always end up being just minor details. They can become dangerous if they end up manifesting in zealous fundamentalism and violence, one of the most notorious incidents of which was the Spanish Inquisition.

Turner's concept of *communitas* is quite similar to Kant's interpretation of how religious solidarity is defined. It is not the universal meaning of the symbol (or, in this case, the Primordial Tradition), but rather how symbols are interpreted and applied to social behavior within a specific community or culture.

> As Kant sees it, genuine religious solidarity does not rest on the confession of a uniform symbol or creed anyway; Kant suspects such creedal formulas of contributing more to a spirit of hypocrisy within people and between them than to anything else. What unites believers in rational religion is not the content of their beliefs but the morality of their dispositions and their propensity to associate their moral vocation with the thought of God.[4]

According to Schuon, the link that connects the many different cultural strands of religious thought is gnosis, or the *philosophia perennis*. Therefore, to fully ascertain how there can be a 'fluid' transmission of gnosis occurring

---

[4] WOOD, A. M., 'Kant's Deism in *Kant's Philosophy of Religion Reconsidered*,' ed. PHILIP J. ROSSI, P. J. & WREEN, M. (Bloomington, IN: Indiana University Press, 1991), 9-10.

between different communities and social groups, a clear definition of gnosis' role is required. Schuon draws a clear distinction between gnosis and sacred scripture, the latter of which he regards as static and permanent:

> The mode of manifestation of gnosis is 'vertical' and more or less 'discontinuous'; it is like fire and not water, in the sense that fire arises from the invisible and can disappear into it again, whereas water has a continuous existence; but the sacred Scriptures remain the necessary and unchanging basis, the source of inspiration and criterion of all gnosis.[5]

Schuon ascribes to gnosis an intangible and fluctuating character, by comparing its qualities to fire. Though teaching and scripture provide fuel and sustenance for gnosis, ultimately the driving power of gnosis is from perennial philosophy and the language of symbolism. Despite the vibrant plethora of symbols used to describe man's inner world through the medium of myth and legend, the exploration of the subconscious via science has only begun to be revitalized in comparatively recent times through the work of psychologists such as Carl Gustav Jung and James Hillman. The work of these men helped revitalize the importance of mythology, religion, and symbolism by examining them from the perspective of a scientist. In essence, they assisted the rediscovery of wisdom, which is the goal of gnosis. These men removed the veil of history to reveal the lost faculty of wisdom. To quote René Guénon,

> [t]ruths which were formerly within reach of all have become more and more hidden and inaccessible; those who possess them grow fewer and fewer, and although

---

5 SCHUON , F., *Gnosis*, 23.

the treasure of 'nonhuman' (that is, supra-human) wisdom that was prior to all the ages can never be lost, it nevertheless becomes enveloped in more and more impenetrable veils, which hide it from men's sight and make it extremely difficult to discover. This is why we find everywhere, under various symbols, the same something which has been lost – at least to all appearances and as far as the outer world is concerned – and that those who aspire to true knowledge must rediscover.[6]

In contemporary Western society, the esoteric aspect of the spiritual traditions has almost disappeared entirely, leaving behind only the exoteric corpus of scripture. It could even be stated that religion itself is dead, or as Friedrich Nietzsche famously proclaimed, *"God is Dead."* However, even this statement is not as atheistic as it appears. It must be interpreted within the context of "The Parable of the Madman" from *The Gay Science*. As such, Nietzsche knew what the consequences of this statement would be. The phrase is a deliberate inversion of the value tables of his time – it is the *devaluation of the highest value*. Nietzsche knew of the existential crisis this 'death' would create in the spiritual life of man and deemed that humankind was not ready to face that event.

As a philosopher dealing with religion and philosophy, Nietzsche also postulated a number of concepts that are not entirely atheistic in sentiment. It is paramount that he must be recognized as an essential critic of religion as well as a philosopher. Primarily, his negative attitude to religion stems from the oppressive Christian environment prevalent in his era. Therefore, it is no coincidence that

---

[6] GUÉNON, R., *The Crisis of the Modern World* (Ghent, NY: Sophia Perennis 2004), 7.

he chose Dionysus as the adversary of the 'Crucified' (Jesus Christ). Despite Nietzsche's negative statements on religion, he frequently draws on mythological symbolism in his writing, including the incorporation of references to figures such as Dionysus, Apollo, and Zarathustra, and he occasionally refers to himself as the 'The Antichrist.' Even without considering Nietzsche's fondness for these colorful characters and archaic pagan Greece, some of his ideas are relevant to the concept of the Primordial Tradition, such as the *Ur-Eine*:

> The *Ur-Eine* – the primal oneness of things [...] Later, the *Ur-Eine* is "another kind of phenomenal world, one which is not knowable to us." But whatever its interpretation at different stages of Nietzsche's development may be, the *Ur-Eine* represents his tortured longing to reach the deeper dimensions of being "which are not known to us."[7]

The concept of the *Ur-Eine* is also similar to the vast *Collective Unconscious* as explored by Carl Jung, an early pioneer in the nascent field of psychology. In terms of Jung's hypothesis concerning the Unconscious and the influence of dreams and symbols upon man's waking life, it is well-known that Jung drew heavily upon mythological sources, applying cross-cultural interpretations to phenomena occurring within the psyche, such as the archetypes. The archetypes are a type of universal (in a manner similar to that espoused by Plato in his interpretation of Universals) which, on the one hand, can be said to contain a purely abstract truth. However, on the other hand, one can also argue that as absolute occurrences of an existential type, the archetypes likewise possess metaphysical significance.

[7] PFEFFER, R., *Nietzsche: Disciple of Dionysus* (Plainsboro, NJ: Associated University Presses, 1977), 116.

Jung himself was quite aware of the fact that his theory placed archetypes in a liminal boundary region between the corporeal and the intangible, and referred to the archetypes as '*psychoids*':

> The archetypes seemed close enough to the patterns he saw emerging in the theories and experiments of twentieth-century physics for him to conclude that archetypes are psychoids. By this, he meant that they shape matter (nature) as well as the mind (psyche). They transcend the split between these two and are neutral toward it, favoring neither one side nor the other.[8]

The archetypes, functioning as what Jung termed as psychoids, operate on the level of 'God-Forms,' as they are symbols of their respective deities. Jung elaborates on this by stating that,

> [w]e know that God-images play a great role in psychology, but we cannot prove the [actual] existence of God. As a responsible scientist, I am not going to preach my personal and subjective convictions, which I cannot prove [...] To me, personally speaking, the question whether God exists at all or not is futile. I am sufficiently convinced of the effects man has always attributed to a divine being. If I should express a belief beyond that...it would show that I am not basing my opinion on facts. When people say they believe in the existence of God, it has never impressed me in the least. Either I know a thing and then don't need to believe it, or I believe it because I'm not sure that I know it. I am well satisfied with the fact that I know

---

[8]   SMITH, H., *Forgotten Truth*, 40.

experiences which I cannot avoid calling numinous or divine.[9]

Therefore, Jung did not base these concepts on a belief in the divine. His ideas were, at least to Jung's line of reasoning, based on verifiable facts that he knew existed. In this regard, the study of archetypes and symbols provide evidence of recurrent ideas that can be empirically verified. The symbol then becomes much more than a pictorial representation of an incident or 'god-form.' First, it is a lesser manifestation of the subject/object represented, and this is the core component for the understanding of sacred art. In the words of Frithjof Schuon,

> [t]he understanding of some symbol is enough to consider the nature of its form. Secondly, its doctrinal, and so traditional, definition, and finally, the metaphysical and spiritual realities of which the symbol is the expression.[10]

It is precisely for this reason that religion and art will always be linked in ways that appear inexplicable. In philosophical circles, it is common to define both art and religion as being devoid of a logical purpose – hence the age-old question, "What is art?" or "What is a religious experience?" However, it is due to their inherent nature that both art and religion are outside of the scope of a purely rational explanation. Any attempt to empirically verify the truthfulness of an artistic endeavor or religious experience will always be met with failure, as is demonstrated below:

---

[9] COTTINGHAM, J., *The Spiritual Dimension: Religion, Philosophy and Human Value* (Cambridge: Cambridge University Press, 2005), 72.

[10] SCHUON, F., *Spiritual Perspectives and Human Facts*, trans. Macleod Matheson (London: Perennial Books, 1969), 63.

Bernard Williams, perhaps the most distinguished analytic moral philosopher writing at the turn of the twentieth century, once speculated that there might be something about ethical understanding that makes it inherently unsuited to be explored through the methods and techniques of analytic philosophy alone. If that is true, the point may apply *a fortiori* to religion, in so far as religious attitudes, even more than moral ones, often seem to encompass elements that are resistant to logical analysis.[11]

Neither the nature of art nor religion can be explained by recourse to empirical measurement alone. This is because the two subjects share an existence in the subconscious as kindred disciplines. The function of art and the function of religion both operate on a level of subliminal aesthetics. A successful artwork can deliver the same experience to that of the divine: it subjects the cognitive processes to a heightened state of emotion that recaptures the original state of the artist or ritual specialist who created it. The emotional sentiment of the creator is replicated in the observer through its transmission, and this determines the success or failure of the art or experience. This is what the Indian philosopher Abhinavagupta also sought to express in his theory of aesthetics, and it correlates to his *rasa* theory.

Notably, we can also find the importance of the "flavor" expressed in the philosophy of David Hume. Nietzsche similarly noted the correspondence between aesthetic and religious experience, concluding that the current path of religion (meaning that which is derived from the relatively modern Judeo-Christian current) was *only one form* that spirituality could have taken. Nietzsche also says that "[a]

---

[11] COTTINGHAM, J., *The Spiritual Dimension,* 1.

rt and not morality is the true metaphysical activity of man."[12] John Cottingham elaborates further on the links between moral and aesthetic experience in his work, *The Spiritual Dimension*:

> Our religious (and moral and aesthetic) experience involves transformative ways of perceiving reality. And this points, incidentally, to something of a paradigm shift when we look, for example, at some of what have been considered traditional arguments for God's existence. Every standard textbook in the philosophy of religion mentions the arguments 'from religious experience,' or 'from moral [aesthetic] experience,' as if what was involved was a kind of inference from one sort of act – roughly a fact about a certain kind of subjective occurrence – to a conclusion about a supposed objective correlate or external cause for the relevant experience.[13]

The topic of the connection between the art of symbols and religious expression is also dealt with at length by Frithjof Schuon:

> In speculations about formal elements, it would be a handicap to lack this aesthetic function of intellect. A religion is revealed, not only by its doctrine, but also by its general form, and this has its own characteristic beauty, which is reflected in its every aspect from its "mythology' to its art. Sacred art expresses reality in relation to a particular spiritual vision. And aesthetic intelligence sees the manifestations of the spirit even as the eye sees flowers or playthings.[14]

---

[12] PFEFFER, R., *Nietzsche: Disciple of Dionysus*, 206.

[13] COTTINGHAM, J., *The Spiritual Dimension*, 85.

[14] SCHUON, F., *Spiritual Perspectives and Human Facts*, 133.

This study of symbols is by no means a simple topic – for Schuon, it is a precise science. Schuon, like other authors before him, connects the mystical experience of the sacred to aesthetics, which he defines as a unique type of intelligence, distinct from other forms of cognition. For Schuon, the interpretation of a symbol as a singular object is insufficient to understand its inherent qualities. Instead, what must be examined in religious semiotics is the relation of the symbol to other qualities, properties, objects, and the context:

> The science of symbols – not simply a knowledge of traditional symbols – proceeds from the qualitative significances of substances, forms, spatial directions, numbers, natural phenomena, positions, relationships, movements, colors and other properties or states of things; we are not dealing here with subjective appreciations, for the cosmic qualities are ordered in relation to Being and according to a hierarchy which is more real than the individual; they are, then, independent of our tastes, or rather they determine them to the extent that we are ourselves conformable to Being; we assent to the qualities to the extent we ourselves are 'qualitative.'[15]

What defines perennial philosophy as the dominant current in the study of religion lies in its use of the symbol and its advocacy of *aesthetic experience*. Faith in the potency of any specific symbol relies upon the most basic human aspect of belief. Belief in a sentient God is not even required. With this explanation of religious belief and symbolism, it is possible for even the most ardent 'atheist' to believe in the power of a symbol or metaphor. In this

---

[15] SCHUON, F., *Gnosis*, 92-93.

regard, it is similar to the thoughts espoused by Kant on Deism:

> Essential to any deism is the view that there is such a thing as rational or natural religion, religion based on natural reason and not on supernatural revelation [...] Kant is emphatic that there need not be any special duties to God in order for there to be religion; he also denies that theoretical cognition of God's existence is required for religion – naturally enough he thinks that no such cognition is available to us.[16] [...] this faith needs merely the idea of God [...] only the minimum cognition (it is possible that there is a God) has to be subjectively sufficient.[17]

A symbol is, of course, only a picture to those who cannot ascertain a deeper meaning. To those who are capable of understanding this code, however, it is reasonable to apply the following quotation: *ex magna luce in intellectu sequitur magna propensio in voluntate* ('from a great light in the intellect there follows a great inclination in the will').[18] It is not satisfactory to develop a rudimentary knowledge of the numinous; this alone is not sufficient to produce gnosis, which in its full manifestation must be grasped at both the level of the theoretical and the practical. The Primordial Tradition of the *sophia perrenis* is composed of ideals from different traditions. It does not advocate a dogmatic system of practice. Instead, it adopts an approach to practice that can be applied to any spiritual tradition. This is similar to the Stoic school

---

[16] WOOD, A. M., 'Kant's Deism in *Kant's Philosophy of Religion Reconsidered*', 7.

[17] Ibid., 8.

[18] COTTINGHAM, J., *The Spiritual Dimension*, 14.

of thought. There were many Stoic treatises entitled 'On Exercises,' but the central notion of *askesis*, as found, for example, in Epictetus, was concerned with the 'art of living.'[19] The importance of *praxis* is in the individual's journey on a path of practical self-transformation, rather than academic rumination or textual analysis.[20]

> The general aim of such programs was not merely intellectual enlightenment, or the imparting of abstract theory, but a transformation of the whole person, including our patterns of emotional response. *Metanoia*, a fundamental conversion or change of heart, is the Greek term; in the Roman Stoic Seneca it appears as a '*shift in one's mentality*' (translatio animi) or a '*changing*' (mutatio) of the self. 'I feel, my dear Lucilius,' says Seneca, 'that I am being not only reformed but transformed (*non tantum emendari sed transfigurari*).'[21]

Huston Smith understood this in his book *The Forgotten Truth,* which was directed at a mainstream audience. Smith claimed that the forms in which the perennial philosophy had existed previously were over-intellectualized, to the point of becoming purely theoretical. By recommending that perennial philosophy should be renamed as the 'Primordial Tradition,' Smith attempted to revitalize what he saw as a failing system of ideology. For him, the reign of the Traditionalist[22] movement was over. Smith realized that a new tactic needed to be deployed in order for the

---

[19] COTTINGHAM, J., *The Spiritual Dimension,* 4.

[20] Ibid., 5.

[21] Ibid., 5.

[22] Traditionalism here refers to the school of philosophy, and not any political movements.

philosophy to extend beyond the reach of an intellectual elite and perforate popular culture. In a sense, Smith attempted to modify the transmission of Tradition itself. This recalls Guénon's warnings that even Traditions can disappear:

> It is evident that all traditional forms do not proceed directly from the primordial tradition and that other forms must have sometimes played the role of intermediaries; but the latter are most often traditions that have entirely disappeared, and those transmissions, in general, go back to epochs far too distant for ordinary history – whose field of investigation is really very limited – to be capable of the slightest knowledge of them, not counting the fact that the means by which they were affected are not among those accessible to its methods of research.[23]

The Primordial Tradition is not a single specific Tradition, but rather an underlying layer of universal truth which acts as a foundation for spiritual traditions to evolve from – and at times dissolve back into. It is the substratum of human subconsciousness itself and defines the nature of epochs and the direction of history, whether man professes to believe in its existence or not.

The quality of the study of spiritual traditions is currently in decline, accompanied by a concurrent deterioration in the academic quality of the arts and the humanities. Under such an aegis, religion – the science of the spirit – needs to be rethought, reshaped, and reconstructed from the very foundations of thought itself to thrive in this era.

---

[23]   GUÉNON, R., *Traditional Forms & Cosmic Cycles* (Ghent, NY: Sophia Perennis 2004), 42.

Perennial philosophy provides a *sui generis* for the translation of symbols from a spiritual perspective. As such, it is apparent that the concept of the Primordial Tradition has more in common with the History of Religions as espoused by Mircea Eliade than it has with the current models of academic debate. In general, however, the study of religion at an academic level is in rapid decline, and the effective approach to the study of spiritual traditions has to therefore occur outside of academia. The only effective solution is to restructure the perennial philosophy, and to change society's rudimentary understanding of *what a spiritual tradition is.*

To quote Huston Smith, there is but one way left to achieve this in the current sociological and political climate: "Short of a historical breakdown which would render routine ineffectual and force us to attend again to things which matter most, we wait for art: for metaphysicians, who, imbued with that species of truth that is beauty in its mental mode, are (like Plato) concomitantly poets."[24]

---

[24]   SMITH, H., *Forgotten Truth: The Primordial Tradition,* 36.

SOPHIA PERENNIS

The Doctrine of Ascension

Humanity's quest for wisdom is as old as the origin of consciousness itself; the inclination towards spirituality and the arts existed as long ago as the dawn of civilization. Deep in the archaic past, culture was born, separating *Homo sapiens* from the other species with whom we share the Earth. Without art and spiritual traditions, there would be no civilization, no progress, and no laws. The advent of spirituality gave rise to art, law, morality, and ethics.

Eventually, the cultural value of spiritual traditions was eroded, replaced by a new and over-zealous faith in the contemporary hyper-capitalist doctrine of 'progress at all costs.' This relentless pursuit of expansion has led to a corresponding interior contraction, resulting in the devastation of the environment, mass extinction of animal life, widespread pollution, and even disease. This naïve belief in the myth of eternal 'progress' is what Dudley Young referred to when he said: "The hand of science, like all human hands, must be recognized as both nurturing and predatory, and the predatory hand must be restrained by laws and prayers to which the heart bears allegiance."[1] Devoid of such restraint, progress can easily lead to

---

[1] YOUNG, D., *Origins of the Sacred: The Ecstasies of Love and War* (London: Little, Brown, and Company Limited, 1992), 23.

29

regression, or worse. Once spiritual beliefs are scorned, culture, humanities, and the arts go into a swift decline, producing a seemingly endless torrent of mediocre works.

Primordial religion was the source of civilization, and it originally provided legislation for society. Spirituality is a universal aspect of the human condition that has been present in our consciousness from the beginning. The Neanderthals practiced the ceremonial burial of their dead, and it is thought that religious ideas first accompanied such rituals about 100,000 years ago.[2] Spiritual traditions, therefore, predate even the origin of our species. Furthermore, if religious practices can be said to have been invented, they have nevertheless managed to infiltrate practically every human civilization, for, as Burkert points out, "religion has never been demonstrably reinvented but has always been there, carried on from generation to generation since time immemorial."[3] Religion and spirituality, therefore, are universal characteristics of human thought, which serve an evolutionary purpose, functioning through the mediums of culture, ethics, and law.

The Primordial Tradition

The primary goal of a true spiritual tradition is to cultivate wisdom.[4] Its secondary goal is soteriological and serves to explain the necessity of death. As sentient beings, humanity is cursed with the knowledge of death's inevitability, and

[2] BURKERT, W., *Creation of the Sacred: Tracks of Biology in Early Religions* (London: Harvard University Press, 1998), 12.

[3] Ibid., 1.

[4] This does not apply to any of the deliberate political distortions of religious or spiritual traditions, and these distortions are often false.

this awareness, as far as we know, is unique to our species. As Emil Cioran once said, "Consciousness is much more than the thorn, it is the dagger in the flesh." Our awareness of death is the dagger that creation thrust into humanity's heart. As such, spiritual traditions have sought, through philosophy and ritual, to bridge the existential rift betwixt life and death, usually in theories of afterlives, souls, immortality, and reincarnation.

Arthur Schopenhauer contended that the purpose of death is to act as a defining point of all genuine religions. Since death is the most traumatic event one can face, it is natural that the mystery of death is humanity's greatest fear. Religion and philosophy are therefore required to explain it, since the empirical methodology of science cannot. It is for this reason that the afterlife plays such a large role in religious belief – for, as the saying goes, "There are no atheists in foxholes." Anyone who has come face-to-face with death or has experienced extreme pain has done so with a humble prayer on their lips. The fear and proximity of death overrides all rational impulses.

This returns us, in an Ouroboros fashion, to the origin of the spiritual traditions, which lies in the Primordial Tradition. As Nicolás Gómez Dávila once wrote on the nature of the sacred, "every innovation is a profanation," implying that every deviation and progression creates distance between a tradition and the purity of its source. Conversely, this places the older traditions closer to the original nature of the sacred. Ultimately, the older and more 'primitive' a tradition is, the purer its connection may be to the nature of the divine.

One author who perceived this was Friedrich Max Müller, the "father of comparative religion."[5] He accepted

---

[5]   MORRIS, B., *Anthropological Studies of Religion: An Introductory*

that a belief in divinity, along with language, formed the basis of cultural identity, writing that "however childish a religion may be, it always represents the highest ideal of perfection which the human soul can reach and grasp."[6] Unlike many scholars of his era, Müller did not believe that 'primitive' traditions were inferior to those in the West. Müller suggested that they possessed an equally valid claim to the numinous. As such, Müller was especially interested in studying the older spiritual traditions to understand the source of religious belief and research its origins. In a sense, therefore, he was searching for *the* Primordial Tradition. Müller was especially attracted to the *Rig Veda* due to its age as a religious text. Müller says that

> [w]e see in the Vedic hymns the first revelation of Deity, the first expressions of surprise and suspicion, the first discovery that behind this visible and perishable world there must be something invisible, imperishable, eternal or divine. No one who has read the hymns of the *Rig Veda* can doubt any longer as to what was the origin [...] names tell us that they were all in the beginning names of the great phenomena of nature, of fire, water, rain, and storm, of sun and moon, of Heaven and Earth.[7]

Venerable traditions like Vedic Hinduism still intrigue both the average reader and the scholar alike – nothing is more mysterious than the beginning, and it is these enigmatic traditions that continue to hold allure, even in modernity, for this is the source of both the sacred

---

Text (Cambridge, MA: Cambridge University Press, 1987), 92.

[6] Ibid., 93.

[7] Ibid., 93-94.

and the divine. The concept of a beginning involves the intersection of the known with the unknown, of existence with non-existence, and this perplexing paradox can prove so daunting that many philosophers have tried to discard it entirely.[8] Both the concept of a beginning and an end suggest a temporal state of emptiness and a chronological infinity, which has to be cyclical, as opposed to the view that 'time' is linear and progressive. For obvious reasons, any confirmation of either is currently outside the scope of empirical verification. The aspect of the older spiritual traditions, which distinguishes them from more modern creations, however, is the pantheistic and henotheist elements, which emphasized the importance of the natural world and provided a teleological model of the sacred. This is the pattern of order in nature to which the universals adhere, offering a teleological model of nature as the mind and body of God. This concept also drew the attention of Max Weber, who writes;

> The process of rationalization favored the primacy of universal gods; and every consistent crystallization of a pantheon followed systematic, rational principles to some degree since it was always influenced by professional sacerdotal rationalism or by the rational striving for order on the part of secular individuals. Above all, it is the aforementioned relationship of a rational regularity of the stars in their heavenly courses, as regulated by divine order, to the inviolable sacred social order in terrestrial affairs, that makes the universal gods the responsible guardians of both these phenomena.[9]

---

[8]   YOUNG, D., *Origins of the Sacred*, 6.

[9]   MORRIS, B., *Anthropological Studies of Religion*, 71.

Weber expands on this statement by elaborating that these ethnic bonds which formulate the basis of the moral and cultural order then develop to formulate prophets (who are distinct from the priests). The latter proceed to rise to power as the heads of religious movements and establish a permanent foundation for a spiritual tradition. A community then naturally arises in connection with the prophetic movement as a result of routinization (*Veralltäglichung*), and the prophet's disciples then secure the permanence of the preaching.[10] It is, therefore, not the organized priesthood who solidifies a tradition, but rather the prophets who act as the *logos* or word of the divine. The priests, once established in the community, then act to consolidate and orchestrate the transmission of the prophet's transmission throughout future generations. A prophet, therefore, does not require the bonds of filiation, which René Guénon believed to be a necessary requirement for belonging to a tradition. Initiation is purely the requirement of mortal law, and *prophets can only be appointed by divine law*. The power of the ancient *ṛṣis*, the bards, magicians, and even the *logos* of Christ were the prophets, who understood the 'secret language of the birds' – esoteric lore, the codified and divine language of symbols.

The Language of the Birds

The language of birds is associated with esoteric wisdom. The most widely-known reference to this secret language occurs in the *Völsunga Saga* when Sigurd acquires the ability to speak it after he slays the dragon Fáfnir. The 'language of the birds' also appears in the traditions of Greece and the Middle East. It is likewise referenced in a

---

[10]   MORRIS, B., *Anthropological Studies of Religion*, 73.

wide range of magical and alchemical texts. The musical dialogue of the birds, who communicate with songs humans do not understand, and through their capacity for flight are able to inhabit the sky and bring them closer to the aethereal dwelling place of the divine, makes both birds and their language an ideal image in esoteric lore.

In terms of language and symbolism, Clifford Geetz continues Weber's ideas, defining religion as being

> (1) a system of symbols which act to (2) establish powerful, persuasive, and long-lasting moods and motivations in men by (3) formulating conceptions of a general order of existence and (4) clothing these conceptions with such an aura of factuality that (5) the moods and motivations seem uniquely realistic.[11]

Émile Durkheim also suggested that sacred objects and emblems were symbols.[12] This is why aesthetics and religion possess an intangible bond: both speak the language of metaphors, which can only be learned via excruciating practice or exceptional innate wisdom. Generally, wisdom accumulates with age and is rare amongst the young. It was for the promulgation of wisdom that spiritual traditions were endowed with social prominence, providing comfort and advice to those in need. As such, religion was primarily educative in its original social function, and only later in history expanded into the codified laws and legislative procedures that still exist today. The difference between modern laws and those of the past, however, is that wisdom is no longer a prerequisite for the practice of law, with legislation now heavily dominated by rigorous bureaucratic procedures.

---

[11] BURKERT, W., *Creation of the Sacred*, 5.

[12] MORRIS, B., *Anthropological Studies of Religion*, 117.

Wisdom, in addition to being acquired through direct experience, is connected to humanity's capacity for creativity, which separates our species from other animals. Leslie White argued, for example, that although chimpanzees are clever animals who can use tools and sign language to express simple emotions and desires, they are fundamentally different from humans in terms of thought.[13] Though apes can paint, they cannot use art to express metaphorical interpretations of reality. Abstraction is a human trait. Therefore, allegorical symbols, as an expression of creativity, can also be an expression of spiritual traditions, for, as Jung states, "the spirit appears in the psyche as instinct."[14] Jung's use of archetypal psychology, later established formally by James Hillman, draws heavily on the nature of symbols, myth, and imagery in order to understand human consciousness. Translating the language of symbols into the nascent field of psychology, Jung says that

> [e]very relationship to the archetype, whether through experience or simply through the spoken word, is "stirring," that is to say, it works because it releases in us a mightier voice than our own. He who speaks in primordial images speaks with a thousand voices; he enthralls and overpowers, while at the same time, he lifts the idea he is trying to express out of the occasional and the transitory into the realm of the ever-enduring. He transmutes our personal destiny into the destiny of mankind, thereby evoking in us all those beneficent forces that ever and anon have

---

[13] WENKE, R. J., *Patterns in Prehistory: Mankind's First Three Million Years* (UK: Oxford University Press, 1990), 77.

[14] Quoting Jung, *On Psychic Energy*. NEUMANN, E., *The Origins and History of Consciousness*, trans. HULL, R. F. C. (Princeton, NJ: Princeton University Press, 1993), 368.

enabled mankind to find a refuge from every peril and to outlive the longest night.[15]

Jung associates archetypes and symbols with representing humanity's creative function. He refers to symbols as "the cocoon of meaning which humanity spins around, and all studies and interpretations of culture are the study and interpretation of archetypes and their symbols."[16] Jung's theory is rooted in Plato's earlier works concerning ideal Forms, which he expanded with the addition of *psychoids*. Jung believed the pyschoids could influence matter (nature) as well as mind (psyche), transcending the schism betwixt the material and the non-material aspects of human life.[17] These pyschoids, like Plato's Forms, act by pouring "direct and luminous intellection into molds – concepts, words, language – that splintered it, for 'rational' and 'ratiocination' presuppose what the words suggest: a process in which we ration or divide up reality into separate things to facilitate discussion."[18] The psychoids define the values associated with them, which in turn compose religion (Latin: *re-ligere* = 'to bind back'): they bind humanity back to historical figures who provided society with traditions and culture.[19] Therefore, the antecedent of religion, the ancestral and communal bond, is the socio-cultural element of spiritual traditions. As Jung says,

---

[15] Ibid., 370.

[16] NEUMANN, E., *The Origins and History of Consciousness*, trans. HULL, R. F. C., 371.

[17] SMITH, H., *Forgotten Truth: The Common Vision of the World's Religions* (San Francisco: Harper, 1992), 40.

[18] Ibid., 66.

[19] YOUNG, D., *Origins of the Sacred,* 18.

[i]t is only possible to live the fullest life when we are in harmony with these symbols; wisdom is a return to them. It is neither a question of belief nor of knowledge, but of the agreement of our thinking with the primordial images of the unconscious. They are the source of all our conscious thoughts, and one of these primordial thoughts is the idea of life after death. Science and these symbols are incommensurables.[20]

The exploration of consciousness now represents the last unexplored frontier for science. However, the thresholds of consciousness, the subconscious, and death are mysteries which at present can only be explained by spiritual traditions. Dealing with death, the soul, and the nature of cognitive experiences are the providence of religions. All authentic spiritual traditions have texts that deal with the experience of death, along with the soteriology that is found in 'doctrines of ascension.' A doctrine of ascension implies that there is an element of existence beyond the human experience of mortality. This element elevates humanity from the mundane world, promising a preternatural way of life. These traditions promise to confer the soul with immortality. However, this afterlife is not accessible to all. There are laws, techniques, and acts which render the ascent possible, closely-guarded teachings that are only bestowed upon the chosen and the faithful. Accordingly, these teachings are only revealed to the most advanced adherents and practitioners.

---

[20] JUNG, C. G., *Modern Man in Search of a Soul*, trans. DELL, W. S., & BAYNES, C. F. (London: Routledge, 2007), 113.

The Body of God

Our life – and consequently, our death – is linked to both the concept of the soul and divinity. In an animist or pantheist tradition, the nature of a god is often inseparable from one or more aspects of the physical. The teleological theory of divinity takes this even further, and the order within nature or the cosmos is seen to be a reflection of the divine. In regard to this, one important author is Charles Hartshorne, whose process theology is more panentheistic than it is pantheistic. Hartshorne defines the relationship between the world and the gods by stating that

> [t]he world consists of individuals which are the constituents of a larger, all-inclusive whole. Like a living creature, this whole is both composite and simple; it exhibits complexity and integrity. When one is speaking of creatures, the emphasis falls upon multitudes of individual components of the world. When one is speaking of God, the emphasis falls upon the unity and singularity of the world. God is the one truly cosmic individual. It follows then that he is the all-encompassing, unencompassed one who is without peer or rival.[21]

This description of divinity and nature draws from earlier traditional sources, and this is particularly so in instances derived from pantheism. In the case of monotheistic traditions, the different facets inherent in nature are absorbed into a singular conception of divinity, which separates the deity from his creation. It is for this reason that the pantheistic traditions have retained a reverence

---

[21]   BILIMORIA, P., *&* STANSELL, E., "Suturing the Body Corporate (Divine and Human) in the Brahmanic Traditions" in *Sophia* (Springer, June 2010), 259.

for the natural world which persists into the contemporary era. These ideas are also prevalent in Hindu texts, since Hinduism is the largest tradition incorporating pantheist ideas. This legacy originated during the Vedic era. For example, in the *Śrīmadbhagavadgītā* (*Bhagavad Gita*) section of the *Mahābhārata*, when Arjuna requests to see Kṛṣṇa's universal form, Kṛṣṇa is revealed as a composite form of divinity with infinite aspects:

> Wearing magnificent garlands and garments, anointed with celestial perfume, consisting entirely of wonders, with faces on all sides. (*Gītā* 11.11)

> If a thousand suns rose all at once in the sky, the collective brilliance of those luminaries might be like the splendor of the Supreme Self. (*Gītā* 11.12)

> [Arjuna] the son of Pāṇḍu saw the whole world, with its various divisions, together there in the body of the god of gods. (*Gītā* 11.13)[22]

This is an extremely ancient line of thought in Hinduism, and it predates even the *Mahābhārata*. It begins in the hymn called the *Puruṣa Sukta*, which relates the story of Puruṣa the Primordial Man.[23] The social divisions in civilization and the three worlds were fashioned out of Puruṣa's form. It is stated that Puruṣa has thousands of bodies, eyes, and feet; enveloping the Earth on all sides, he extends beyond it by ten finger-breadths.[24] All order originates from Puruṣa, the body of the larger organism, serving to illustrate how the parts integrate into society and allows the cosmos to function as a whole.

---

[22] Ibid., 243-244.

[23] Ibid., 239-240.

[24] Ibid.

From his mouth were made the *brāhmaṇas*, from his arms the *rājanyas*.

From his thighs were born the *vaiśyas*, from his feet the *śūdras*.

The moon was born from his mind, the sun from his eye.

Indra and Agni emerged from his mouth. From his vital breath was born the air.

From his navel came the intermediate space, from his head heaven.

From his feet came the Earth, from his ears the four quarters. Thus were the three realms created.[25]

Everywhere, the divine is present in nature, since Puruṣa, the universal intellect, permeates all aspects of *Prakṛti*, or nature.[26] This idea is found in other aspects of Hinduism, particularly in the figure of Prajāpati. The god Dakṣa is used as a substitute for Prajāpati in the Purāṇas. Both deities are personifications of the cosmic order and the cosmogonic sacrifice to the gods, which perpetuates the *dharman* (human law) and *ṛta* (cosmic law) that sustain *dharma, karma*, and the fabric of existence. In this capacity, Prajāpati is strongly associated with the creative function. Both Prajāpati and Dakṣa transgress against the *ṛta* themselves, at which point they were punished by the gods Rudra and Śiva respectively. As 'outsider deities,' only these two gods can function beyond *dharma's* effects, and

---

[25] Ibid.

[26] DANIÉLOU, A., *Shiva and Primordial Tradition: From the Tantras to the Science of Dreams*, trans. HURRY, K. F., (Vermont: Inner Traditions 2007), 3.

are able to administer punishment. Although Dakṣa and Prajāpati represent cosmic order, they remain bound by the laws of order and can be reprimanded by the 'outsider deities' who, despite being unrestrained, still uphold the law. Prajāpati and Dakṣa are both the ritual specialists and the ritual sacrifice. Prajāpati's connection to the nature and role of sacrifice is described as follows:

> Prajāpati emitted (i.e., brought into existence) the creatures (offspring, living beings) [...] The process is obviously viewed as an exteriorization (or obtainment of independent existence) of (a) being(s) or object(s) that hitherto was (were), or might be supposed to be, within the creator, to form part of the totality that was his being or person. In a similar way, Prajāpati is often briefly stated to have emitted from himself sacrificial worship.[27]

Prajāpati is not just the sacrifice's original performer. He is also described *as the sacrifice itself* – "Prajāpati (is the) *yajña*."[28] The significance of Prajāpati's cosmogonic rites also extends into texts such as the *Cāndogya Upaniṣad* and hymns in the *Rig* and *Sama* Vedas, which are said to constitute the human body.[29] Tantrism likewise incorporates sacred topology where geological features are associated with deities, and this is explicitly associated with Dakṣa's opposition to Śiva, as a number of these features are identified with the Devī, whose body parts fall to the land at the conclusion of the incident with Dakṣa.

---

[27] GONDA, J., "Vedic Gods and the Sacrifice" in *Numen*, Vol. 30, Fasc. 1. (Brill, 1983), 3.

[28] Ibid., 6.

[29] Ibid., 242.

In terms of the ritual aspect, when performed by humans the sacrificer's Ātman is identical with Prajāpati, and he shares both the identity of God and the sacrifice.[30] Seen in this light, the distinction between the rite and the participant is a reflection of the relationship between Brahman (the creator, world ground, and inner self of all beings) and Ātman (the self or soul). The human body, the sacrifice, is a physical representation of the sacrifice, which serves as a medium to homologize the schism between Brahman and Ātman, between the microcosm of the individual (mortal) and the macrocosm of the cosmos (divine). Parallels with this idea are also found in other spiritual traditions.

Thomas McEvilley suggests that the hypotheses of Plato's *Parmenides* are analogous to this concept, stating that "Plato's One, Demiurge, and Indefinite Dyad (the passive, material principle) correspond to Puruṣa, Tgvara, and Prakṛti, respectively."[31] Similarities to Puruṣa can also be seen in the death of the Norse Ymir, who is reformed into the Earth, but the creative function belongs to Oðinn, who bestows his gift of ǫnd (breath, spirit, soul) to the first man and woman.[32]

The soul is often identified with breath; even today, the basic test in First Aid to demonstrate life is the persistence of breath. Where there is breath, there is also life. In the world of spiritual tradition, the breath and the life are one and the same – we could almost even say, "*The breath is the life.*" The Greeks called this breath *phusis,* and Henri

---

[30] Ibid., 19.

[31] BUSSANICH, J., "The Roots of Platonism and Vedanta: Comments on Thomas McEvilley" in *International Journal of Hindu Studies 9,* 1-3 (World Heritage Press Inc, 2005), 15.

[32] AULD, R. L., "The Psychological and Mythic Unity of the God Odinn" in *Numen,* Vol. 23, Fasc. 2. (Brill, 1976), 154-155.

Bergson called it the *élan vital*.[33] Part of the reasoning behind this association in Hellenic Tradition originates with Anaximenes, who had declared that "air is the principle (*arche*) of existing things: for from it all things come to be, and into it, they are again dissolved" and "air, holds us together and controls us, so does wind (or breath) and air enclose the whole world."[34] The idea of correlating air with life or breath also connects it with *aither* (*aithō* = to burn, blaze), which implies it is "pure or clear air."[35] Aither was similarly mentioned by Isaac Newton in his *Second Paper on Light and Colours*, where he wrote that

> [p]erhaps the whole frame of nature may be nothing but various contextures of some certain aitherial spirits. Thus perhaps may all things be originated from aither.[36]

This statement reinforces the likelihood that Isaac Newton, at least on a subconscious level, harbored sentiments similar to the Greeks.

The idea of the soul is also intimately entwined with the teleological model of the microcosm and the macrocosm. The realization that the two are one, and the consequential attempts to homologize them, are found in a diverse range of spiritual traditions. The realization of the relationship between Ātman and Brahman is, therefore, one of the highest soteriological value.[37]

---

[33] YOUNG, D., *Origins of the Sacred*, 30.

[34] MIHAI, A., "Soul's Aitherial Abode According to the Poteidaia Epitaph and the Presocratic Philosophers" in *Numen* 57 (Brill, 2010), 565.

[35] Ibid., 554.

[36] Ibid., 554.

[37] BILIMORIA, P., & STANSELL, E., "Suturing the Body Corporate

Similar ideas are found in *Timaeus*, including the fact that the cosmos is rendered as an ensouled body, qualifying as a living being.[38] *Timaeus* declares that the cosmos was generated as a living being endowed with soul and intelligence.[39] Plato's *Republic* depicts the soul as being tripartite – consisting of the rational, the spirited, and the appetitive parts – which correspond to three distinct regions (head, heart, and lower abdomen) that service the soul.[40] Furthermore, Plato states that

> [e]very *psuchê* [soul] is immortal. For what is ever-moving is immortal. Every body whose movement comes from without is inanimate (*apsuchos*), and every body whose movement comes from within is animate (*empsuchos*), this being the nature of an animator (*psuchê*). And if this is so, and if what moves itself is nothing other than an animator, then from necessity, animators will be both ingenerated and immortal.[41]

These ideas on the soul naturally raised the question of what happened to the soul after death. If it is immortal, then the soul must somehow depart the flesh and journey on elsewhere, which required an explanation. Furthermore, it also raised the question of whether or not the soul could depart from a living a body – either

---

(Divine and Human) in the Brahmanic Traditions," 243.

[38] PLATO, *Timaeus & Critias*, trans. JOHANSEN, T. K. (London: Penguin Classics, 2008), xxiv.

[39] SALLIS, J., *Chorology: On Beginning in Plato's Timaeus* (Bloomington, IN: Indiana University Press, 1999), 58.

[40] PLATO, *Timaeus & Critias*, xxvi.

[41] MIHAI, A., "Soul's Aitherial Abode According to the Poteidaia Epitaph and the Presocratic Philosophers," 566.

voluntarily or involuntarily. The Greeks attempted to answer these questions through pneumatic experiments, in which attempts were made to extract the soul from a living body. These experiments were usually performed on young boys, who were deemed to be morally pure, for in youth, the soul was perceived to be free from corruption. Proclus, in his commentary on Plato's myth of Er, states the following:

> That the soul can leave the body and return to it is shown by the story about the man of whom Clearchus says that he used his hypnotizing rod (*psuchulkoi rhabdoi*) on a sleeping young man, so that the revered Aristotle, too, became convinced, as Clearchus describes in his work *On Sleep*, that the soul can separate from the body and that it enters the body and uses it as its dwelling-place. For by touching the young man with his rod, he caused the soul to depart, and while he led it away from the body by this means, he demonstrated that the body was motionless but remained unharmed, though insensible to blows as if inanimate. But after the rod had brought back the soul, which had meanwhile stayed outside the body, close to the body, it re-entered and could tell everything.[42]

This led to other theories concerning metempsychosis (a form of reincarnation) which deal with the transmigration of the soul. Regarding the origin of the doctrine of metempsychosis, Herodotus of Halicarnassus claimed metempsychosis originated in Egypt and was introduced to Greece by the Pythagoreans. Herodotus stated that the Egyptians were also the first to advance the theory that the soul of man is immortal and that when the "body perishes

---

[42] MIHAI, A., "Soul's Aitherial Abode According to the Poteidaia Epitaph and the Presocratic Philosophers," 572.

GWENDOLYN TAUNTON

it enters into (*eisduesthai*) another living creature which comes into being at that moment, and when it has gone round all the land animals and all the sea animals and all the birds, it enters again into the body of a man who is coming into being; and this circumambulation goes on for three thousand years."[43] There are also texts which record events similar to metempsychosis occurring amongst the living, and it is usually associated with the induction of an altered state of consciousness and prophetic ability. One such description is the soul journey of Aristeas of Proconnesus:

> As he lay on the ground, scarcely breathing, his soul, abandoning his body, wandered like a bird and saw everything beneath it: Earth, sea, rivers, towns, the customs and passions of mankind, and natures of every kind. Then, returning to its body and making it rise, using it once again as an instrument, it told what it had seen and heard.[44]

In accounts such as this, the soul is believed to be capable of separating from the living physical body, leading to the creation of what can be termed the 'astral' or 'illusory' body, which exists in a semi-detached state of bilocational consciousness. One account of this separation of the soul from the body is related by Tertullian when he speaks of the mystical abilities of Hermotinus:

> With regard to the case of Hermotimus, they say that he used to be deprived of his soul in his sleep as if it wandered away from his body like a person on a holiday trip. His wife betrayed the strange peculiarity.

---

[43] Ibid., 569.

[44] MIHAI, A., "Soul's Aitherial Abode According to the Poteidaia Epitaph and the Presocratic Philosophers," 573.

47

His enemies, finding him asleep, burnt his body as if it were a corpse: when his soul returned too late, it appropriated (I suppose) to itself the guilt of the murder.[45]

Both Aristotle and Plato believed that the soul was inactive while the body was awake and active when the body was asleep. Generally, it was assumed among the Greeks that the soul could only leave the body once it was in a restful state of either trance or sleep. It is for this reason that Hypnos (Sleep) and Thanatos (Death) are both the children of Nyx (Night). Similarly, both the origin of dreams and the resting place of the dead were located in the Chthonic realm of Hades. This indicates that the Greeks believed dreams and death were connected. The following verse, quoted by Plato in *Meno,* also illustrates this connection:

In happy fate all die a death
that frees from care,
and yet there still will linger behind
a living image of life (*aionos eidolon*),
for this alone has come from the gods.
It sleeps while the members are active;
but to those who sleep themselves
it reveals in myriad visions
the fateful approach
of adversities or delights.[46]

Plato refers not only to death here but also to the Greek practice of dream incubation (entering the liminal dream-state) and divination (oneiromancy) to predict future

[45] Ibid., 573.

[46] MIHAI, A., "Soul's Aitherial Abode According to the Poteidaia Epitaph and the Presocratic Philosophers, 576.

events.[47] This, however, does not explain what happens to the soul after death. This can be explained by reading Euripides:

> Now let the dead be laid in Earth, and each part return thither whence it came into the light of day, the breath into the aither of Heaven, the body into Earth. For the body is not ours in fee; we are but lifelong tenants; and after that, Earth that nursed it must take it back again.[48]

The soul retains its association with the aither while the physical form returns to the Earth. This association of aither with the celestial realm dates back to the time of Homer and Hesiod, where Zeus was said to live in the aither: "Zeus, most glorious, most great, lord of the dark clouds who dwells in the aither."[49] This is also reiterated in the *Epitaph of Poteidaia* where it is written, "Aither has taken their souls, and earth their bodies."[50] Due to its nature, the soul aspires towards the aither, whereas the body, because of its material form, returns to the Earth.[51] Therefore, a dichotomy is created in soteriology; there are two paths to the afterlife: one in the Uranic aither, the other in the Chthonic Earth. This is also paralleled by Heraclitus' theory of exhalations according to which the bright exhalation of souls goes to the Sun, producing day and summer, and the dark exhalation of souls goes to

---

[47] BUSSANICH, J., "The Roots of Platonism and Vedanta," 13.

[48] MIHAI, A., "Soul's Aitherial Abode According to the Poteidaia Epitaph and the Presocratic Philosophers," 558.

[49] Ibid., 562-563.

[50] Ibid., 556.

[51] Ibid., 558.

the Moon, producing night and winter.[52] This does not, however, evoke the same moral judgment as Christianity. The domain of Hades was not equivalent to the Christian Hell, and rather than being a realm reserved for 'sinners' was, instead, simply a resting place for the ordinary dead. The Uranic paradise in the aither, by contrast, was much more difficult to enter. It was reserved for those who had become 'more than human' and transcended the mortal condition. This is expressed in Plato's *Timaeus*, where it clearly says that the ordinary souls "return unperfected and unmindful to Hades."[53]

This archaic separation of the cosmic dyad is almost universal in humanity. This is an elaboration on the great *hieros gamos*, which refers to the marriage between the physical Heaven and Earth.[54] However, in the incorporeal world of the soul, it becomes the celestial Uranic pole and the subterranean Chthonic pole, both of which do not possess a physical form in the same manner that the sky and Earth possess. These are the two poles of the *axis mundi*, which hold the domain of humanity in between. The corrected triad then becomes Uranic, Telluric, and Chthonic.

Similarly, Hinduism has three components: Heaven (*dyava*), Earth (*prthivi*), and the mid-space (*antarika*).[55] Thus is our 'world' located between the celestial and the domain below ground on the vertical plane of ascent and descent, at the sacred center of the cosmos. Obviously,

[52]   BUSSANICH, J., "The Roots of Platonism and Vedanta," 3.

[53]   SALLIS, J., *Chorology,* 88.

[54]   ELIADE, M., *The Sacred and the Profane: The Nature of Religion* (New York: Harcourt, Brace & World, Inc., 1959), 169.

[55]   KRAMRISCH, S., "The Triple Structure of Creation in the Rg Veda," *History of Religions,* Vol. 2, No. 1 (University of Chicago, 1962), 144.

these are not physical locations but rather different polarities derived from psychological states. Betwixt the two poles, there is no inferiority or superiority, nor do they equate with ethical judgments such as 'good and evil.' There is only a difference of perspective: not all souls will seek reunion with the divine, preferring to remain in the terrestrial cycle of rebirth until they become desirous of release, or *mokṣa,* as it is called in Hinduism.

In the Vedic Tradition, Heaven is the domain of the Vedic deity Savitṛ, who represents the higher aspects of solar symbolism. Savtṛ the Impeller or Vivifier is distinct from Surya, however, who represents the physical aspect of the Sun. Savitṛ, by contrast, represents creative power, intelligence, and the higher aspects of cognition. The subterranean world is under the dominion of the deity Yama. Yama, as a ruler of the Underworld, has more in common with gods such as Hades and Hel, rather than the Christian Satan, who acts as a mere administrator of punishment. An extract from the *Rig Veda* serves to clarify that Yama is not equivalent to the Christian figure of Satan:

> Three [are] the heavens, two [are] the lap of Savitṛ, one [is] in the world of Yama, the ruler of men. This one heaven is here in this world ruled over by death, the other heavens are the light worlds, the lap of Savitṛ, the Impeller who keeps this creation moving.[56]

The domain of Yama is therefore merely a different afterlife, just as it was in the Greek tradition. It is also worth noting that Yama is referred to here as the ruler of the human world. This is because all mortal creatures, due to their finite lifespans, are subject to the rule of death,

---

[56] Ibid., 153.

and this concept is found even in the later Iranian echoes of the original Vedic Tradition.

Though the Christian Hell does not equate with the Chthonic realm, there are other horrors lurking, at least for now, in the primordial darkness. Rather, the true mythos of 'evil' takes on a different form, in an eternal void of pure chaos that exists beyond the domain of cosmic order. Here, in the primeval abyss, humanity's oldest and deepest fears survive, gnawing at the roots of the rational mind and conjuring unimaginable terrors from the corners of the universe, where no laws exist. Here, in the sunless chasm, we find Vṛta the Serpent. Outside of Hinduism, this Great Serpent has many names: Tiamat, Níðhöggr, and countless more. Vṛta, existing as chaos, is the symbol of *anṛta*, the inchoate adversary of order. The dark spaces where the Serpent was said to dwell exist beyond cosmic law:[57]

> The source of *ṛta*, of cosmic order, is in the realm of the *Asura*, the Father, beyond creation. In this dark space of no distinction, all is flood. But when the child of Fire, Hiraṇyagarbha, the Son of the Waters, Apām Nāpat, Agni in his secret nest will be fledged, spread his wings and let his light shine in the cosmos, the *Sat*, the existent, norm and order (*ṛta*) will flow into it from the source. But a tremendous obstacle had to be overcome before the waters of creation could flow into the cosmos. Sleeping, it blocked their way, enclosed and covered them altogether with its dark power. This power is the Serpent Vṛta, the Coverer. Vṛta enclosed the realm of the Father, obstructed creativeness. Vṛta had grown in sunless darkness. He enclosed these two great conjoint worlds-to-be, Heaven and Earth, the monad-to-be, he enclosed the neither-nor of the

---

[57] Ibid., 273.

unfathomable deep waters when there was neither space nor Heaven above it. Vṛta was to be split and felled by Indra, the god of a new dispensation, Liberator of the waters and Creator of the cosmos, the king of the world.[58]

The Serpent is an obvious metaphor for the subconscious animal impulse that represents the fear of our dark inner depths – it is a cold-blooded, venomous predator that hides until it is ready to strike its prey. Vṛta is the darkness that obscures reason with abject fear, negating all creative functions and the laws which originate from them – even cosmic ones. As such, the Serpent represents pure unimaginable cosmic terror. The waters represent the fluid nature of the subconscious, the recesses of the mind where the Serpent basks, unseen in their depths. It is to Vṛta that evil-doers and those who intentionally twist words or distort the truth are delivered.[59] As Vṛta, the arch-enemy, the Serpent (*ahi*) whom Indra killed, the creator of our world, lay on the ground of the dark space (*rajaso budhnam asayat*), he blocked the waters so that they could not flow into creation but remain in the undifferentiated wholeness of the flood.[60] Thus, when Indra slew Vṛta the consciousness and the power of reason in it was unleashed as the magical power of creation, which enabled humanity to build civilization. This myth is nothing less than the transition of man from a biological organism alone to a sentient and rational deity. It is the struggle of the conscious against the subconscious and a mythological depiction of the dawn of awareness in the archaic beginning of primordial time.

---

[58] Ibid., 272.

[59] Ibid., 275.

[60] Ibid.

Still connected with the power of the subconscious, the Serpent, in its second incarnation as Ahi Budhnya, continues to live in the waters, but is now subject to the will of the gods and Order, functioning within the confines of a creative role. Down in the depths, Ahi Budhnya is unable to create and instead listens to the songs of the poets, approving and blessing them – or inflicting harm and punishment, destroying, or sanctioning everything that is created.[61] The Serpent, instead of attacking the creative power, is now relegated to a new role: judging the creative power of mortals, chiding them for poor aesthetic choices, and functioning as the ultimate art critic.

****

Ascension to the aither directs the soul to a celestial or Uranic path. A descent to the Chthonic Underworld procures a tranquil repose in the afterlife and a possible rebirth in the Telluric domain of humankind. To bypass the cycle of metempsychosis or reincarnation, one must overcome the human condition. However, to overcome the limitations of human existence and acquire 'liberation,' one must first utilize innate wisdom or devote himself to ritual practice. Those who manage to ascend the mortal condition escape the cycle of rebirth and are reunited with the divine. Thus, the acceptance of Order, and that of ṛta, is implicated as a condition for the ascent. It is explicitly stated that one gains immortality only by accruing wisdom or via ritual practice, as is stated in the following:

Death spoke to the Gods: "Now surely all men will be immortal. What will be my share?" They said, "From

---

[61] Ibid., 276.

now on, no one will become immortal with the body. Only when you have taken that as your share will he become immortal, either through ritual (*karman*) or knowledge (*vidyā*)."[62]

This passage clearly states that only wisdom/knowledge or ritual practice can provide one with an immortal afterlife. Furthermore, it also implies that this afterlife is not egalitarian or accessible to all, as is the case in Christian doctrine. Rather, it favors the wise and the ritual specialists.

Immortality cannot be achieved physically. Therefore, for immortality to be possible, one must overcome the burden of the flesh and become detached from the physical body. Without a 'soul' or 'individual consciousness' that is capable of separation from the body, any form of personal immortality is completely impossible. As a solution to this problem, human divinity (*daiva ātman*) is believed to be achievable through the power of ritual work. One can win "the 'world of men' (*mānuṣya loka*); that is, he realizes his potentialities are gaining access to a 'heavenly world' (*svarga loka*) that he inhabits after death."[63] The soul, in this regard, can also be regarded as a ritual construct in a similar fashion to the cosmogonic ritual construct of Prajapati/Dakṣa. Ritual, therefore, can transform the individual participant into a new divine form:

The sacrifice becomes the sacrificer's *ātman* in yonder world. And, truly, the sacrificer who, knowing this, performs that [sacrifice] comes into existence with a

[62] SMITH, B. K., "Gods and Men in Vedic Ritualism: Toward a Hierarchy of Resemblance" in *History of Religions*, Vol. 24, No.4 (University of Chicago Press, May 1985), 296.

[63] Ibid., 299.

whole (*sarva*) body [...] his ritual accomplishments
on Earth the precise measure of his *daiva ātman*.[64]

The goal of the sacrifice, then, is to procure immortality in
the celestial world by obtaining a divine self in that world
after death.[65] To initiate the process of ascent, the ritual
participant sometimes identifies with the form of a bird.
The Hindu fire altar was originally represented as a bird,
and similar imagery is seen in various spiritual traditions,
for the power of flight is a universal symbol of ascension.
In the case of the Hindu altar, it is the *yajña* that is
regarded as a bird.[66] Brahmin priests were regarded as
human gods (*mānuṣya devas*) and were to be propitiated
in the sacrifice along with other divinities:

> There are two kinds of gods. For the gods [are gods]
> and the Brahmins who have studied and teach are
> human gods. The sacrifice of these [sacrificers] is
> divided into two: oblations [are sacrifices] to the
> gods and sacrificial fees [are sacrifices] to the human
> gods, the Brahmins who have studied and teach. With
> oblations, one pleases the gods, with sacrificial fees
> one pleases the human gods, the Brahmins who have
> studied and teach. Both these kinds of gods, when
> pleased, place him in a condition of well-being.[67]

Ascension to the Uranic realm also plays a part in sacred
rulership. One needs to distance themselves from the
human world in order to access the Uranic one, and make
the required sacrifice, which "has its only [true] foundation

---

[64] Ibid., 304.

[65] Ibid., 292.

[66] Ibid., 293.

[67] Ibid., 291-292.

(*pratiṣṭha*), its one [true] end (*nidhana*)."[68] Furthermore, the transitional phase is inordinately difficult. In the case of the royal sacrificer, during the "*rājasūya* sacrifice the king must 'go to the world of heaven' first but then be sure to return to the Earth, which is his 'firm foundation.'"[69]

> In that he is consecrated by the *rājasūya* he ascends to the world of Heaven. If he did not descend to this world, he would either depart to a region which lies beyond [all] human beings, or he would go mad. In that, there is that sacrifice for shaving the hair [the *keśavapanīya*] with reversed chants, [this serves] for not leaving this world. Just as he would descend [from a tree], grabbing branch after branch, so he descends by this [rite] to this world. [It serves, then] for attaining a firm foundation.[70]

This power to travel to the Uranic (or Chthonic) realm is also associated with magico-religious techniques and the acquisition of occult power. As such, the Hindu *siddhis* operate by deploying magic as an active force on corporeal matter, in a similar manner to the *psychoids*.[71]

All traditions themselves agree on how this is to be done, but the ascent is almost unanimously associated with flight. In the case of the king, he first ascends to gain knowledge and then returns to the Earth to provide wise guidance for the benefit of the kingdom.

To 'fly' to the celestial, however, first entails the soul's ability to exit the body. There are numerous descriptions of this process in spiritual traditions, often utilizing the

---

[68] Ibid., 296.

[69] Ibid., 306.

[70] Ibid., 297.

[71] SMITH, H., *Forgotten Truth*, 41.

imagery of a tower, house, the head/skull – or an upper opening that makes passage to another world possible. For example, the upper opening of an Indian tower bears, among other names, that of *brahmarandhra*, which also designates the opening at the top of the skull.[72] In Hindu thought, the *Arhat,* who "breaks the roof of the house" and flies away through the air, demonstrates that the Arhat has transcended mortality and attained a higher state of Being.[73] Buddhist texts also refer to Arhats, who "fly through the air and break the roof of the palace," and who, "flying by their own will, break and pass through the roof of the house and travel through the air."[74] In proto-historic China and Etruria, funerary urns were made in the shape of a house and possessed an opening at the top to permit the dead man's soul to enter and leave.[75]

Similar imagery is found in Tibetan Buddhism. In the advent of death, the family of the dying person would request a Lama to perform the *phowa* ceremony, or the transference of consciousness, at the time of death.[76] *Phowa* is an esoteric technique that is passed on solely as an oral tradition. However, some records pertaining to its practice can be found in texts such as the *Six Yogas of Naropa* (and the *Six Yogas of Niguma*). References to *phowa* are also carefully concealed in the *Tibetan Book of the Dead. Phowa* is linked to the practice which enables the Dalai Lama to reincarnate, which is why it is one of the

---

[72] ELIADE, M., *The Sacred and the Profane*, 174.

[73] Ibid., 176.

[74] Ibid., 175.

[75] Ibid., 179.

[76] "The Teaching of Phowa (Transference of Consciousness at the Time of Death) According to the Teaching of the Patul Rinpoche in the *Kunsang Lami Shellung*," from *Internet Sacred Text Archive* (www.sacred-texts.com/bud/tib/phowa.htm).

most closely-guarded secrets of the Buddhist Tradition. *Phowa* is believed to be so potent that even the most corrupted souls can achieve liberation through it:

> Even if a man is so sinful that he kills a holy man every day and has committed the five Heavy Sins, if he goes on this path of *phowa* the veils of sin will not remain. For the men of many sins and for all beings, this is the Path of liberation which is direct and secret.[77]

The exit point for the soul is, again, located at the top of the skull. Above the nine ordinary apertures of the body called *buga*, there is a crest aperture, and this aperture enables the soul to exit the body at the time of death, where it is then directed to an afterlife in Dewachen (Blissful Land).[78] Physically, this site corresponds to the suture formed by the parietal bones at the top of the skull known as the saggital suture. It is also represented in Yogic-Tantric tradition by the *Sahasrara Chakra*. Interestingly enough, this aperture is found within Hermeticism and the Egyptian Tradition as well, where the soul is represented as winged Sun atop the caduceus. This is another symbol of ascension and represents the combined power of the Uranic and Chthonic currents, which is mastered by control of both the solar and lunar channels.

It is the liberation of the soul from the body which enables one to achieve immortality in the afterlife, and this is not based strictly on morality or ethics, but on the perfection of practices within the respective spiritual traditions.

In the Abrahamic traditions, where only a Uranic afterlife is promulgated and the Chthonic afterlife has

[77] Ibid.

[78] Ibid.

been transformed into 'Hell', the ascent of the soul is often depicted by images of a bridge and a narrow gate, implying that it is a dangerous passage. Although no physical exit from the body is mentioned, initiation, mysticism, and faith in the Abrahamic traditions are all mechanisms of the ascent.[79] Similarly, in earlier Middle Eastern mythology, the Cinvat Bridge for the dead "is nine lance-lengths wide for the just, but for the wicked, it becomes as narrow as 'the blade of a razor' and the mystics always pass over this bridge on their ecstatic journeys to Heaven."[80] The *Vision of St. Paul* likewise describes a bridge to the celestial world, which is as "narrow as a hair." Medieval legends similarly tell of sword bridge, which Lancelot has to "cross barefoot and with bare hands"; it is "sharper than a scythe" and is crossed in "pain and agony."[81] This is nearly identical to a myth in the Finnish Tradition, which describes a bridge covered with needles, nails, and razor blades that the dead use to journey to the other world.[82]

****

Science alone cannot explain the frontiers of human consciousness, as these aspects of cognitive function cannot yet be measured or defined purely with the empirical method. This is not to erect a false dichotomy between science and spiritual traditions, but rather to demonstrate that the balance between the material sciences and the science of the spirit should be harmonious rather than antagonistic, as is the case with psychology. In this field, one can deal with both scientific

[79] ELIADE, M., *The Sacred and the Profane*, 181.

[80] Ibid., 181-182.

[81] Ibid., 182.

[82] Ibid.

facts and converse in the language of symbols to discuss the inner experiences of man, as religion once did. Archetypal psychology in particular incorporates a deep understanding of mythology and ancient wisdom, while operating under the aegis of science. One of the founding figures of psychology, Carl Jung, acknowledged that the loss of man's interior life was a tragedy, stating that

> [t]he spiritual problem of modern man is one of those questions which belong so intimately to the present in which we are living that we cannot judge of them fully. The modern man is a newly formed human being; a modern problem is a question which is a question which has just arisen and whose answer lies in the future.[83]

Modern man is not the same as Traditional man; the inner security provided by cultural and spiritual ties is gone. Today people strive to discover their essence, the individual nature of *Being*, but fail and become lost in a vast population of others who are all seeking their own individuality. Thus, one can feel alone, even when surrounded by people, isolated in a new digital age. The complexity of modern life makes it difficult for some to establish their own individual role so that they cannot obtain a sense of Being, and without this, no ascent is possible. This sentiment is echoed by the last of the true perennial philosophers, Huston Smith:

> Even the addict who prowls the streets for his angry "fix" and the assassin who stalks his fated prey are reaching out for being. The alleys that they walk are blind ones; judged in terms of the larger being they

---

[83] JUNG, C. G., *Modern Man in Search of a Soul*, 200.

preclude or the damage they work on the being of others, they stand condemned. But if it were possible to consider the cocaine's "rush" by itself, apart from its consequences, it would be judged good; the same holds for the satisfaction that sweeps over the assassin as he effects his revenge. *Esse qua esse bonum est.* Being as being is good; more being is better.[84]

Lack of Being, the desire to express the soul, extends to other aspects of existence: art becomes a medium for self-expression rather than individual skill, drugs are utilized to escape the horror of an empty existence, and even crime becomes an expression of Being and an act of protest against the modern world. The spiritual root crisis of the modern world stems from this loss of Being. Loss of Being equates to the loss of the soul, and eventually, to loss of human nature itself. Cultural and social breakdown inevitably follow suit. What begins with one individual, spreads to affect an entire group.

Not caring about the past and unable to conceive the future, *homo modernus* is in danger of becoming a creature of the moment, forever seeking an external stimulus to fulfill a hollow interior. The true self or soul is lacking, and all prospect for ascension is consequently negated. By denouncing the soul, one severs one's link to the macrocosm, rendering oneself unable to perform the role that is required for them to achieve entry to the celestial Uranic afterlife. In this state of nihilism, it is not surprising that the modern world denounces the existence of anything beyond the physical. Likewise, it is not surprising that the Chthonic afterlife, through a long process of misunderstanding, was distorted into a Hell for 'sinners,' while simultaneously making it possible for even

---

[84] SMITH, H., *Forgotten Truth*, 77.

the worst criminals to enter Heaven if they merely ask for forgiveness. This is a consequence of incomplete spiritual transmissions, which have been passed on minus the doctrines of ascension. As such, the Uranic and Chthonic poles were reconceptualised as moral absolutes instead of possessing the bifurcated soteriological functions they held in earlier periods of history, when they occupied higher levels of symbolic abstraction.

The crisis of Being and the soul will define the twenty-first century as we encounter a new world, which for the first time in centuries will see a great decline in both the quality of material life and the diminishing of social security around the world. Once material comforts become out of financial reach for many, we will need care and nurturing from the creative and cultural worlds which will also entail a revival of spiritual traditions. As Erich Neumann says, "The turning of the mind from the conscious to the unconscious, the responsible approach of human consciousness with the powers of the collective psyche, that is the task of the future."[85]

Homini enim impressa est imago Dei, ut in ea luceat et agnoscatur Deus.

---

[85] NEUMANN, E., *The Origins and History of Consciousness*, 393.

ESOTERIC TRADITIONS

ARS REGIA

Alchemy & the Primordial Tradition

Yathā tathā dehe
As in metal, so in the body
—*The Ocean of Mercury*

The Royal Art, or Ars Regia, more commonly known as alchemy, is sometimes a controversial area of research. This is so primarily for two reasons. Firstly, alchemy is viewed by some as a primitive precursor to chemistry. The alchemists employed obscure scientific terminology to describe certain principles, the true meaning of which was being hidden from the general public at that time. They also often expressed themselves in metaphors in order to disguise the true nature of their work. This has misled many a historian into concluding that alchemy is nothing more than a rudimentary form of chemistry. However, when read in an appropriate context, alchemy is revealed to be a metaphysical process dealing with purely spiritual principles.

The second controversial issue occurs when it becomes necessary to define what alchemy actually is. With this quest for a definition in mind, should alchemy be regarded as a complete tradition, or is it a component of other traditions, such as the Chinese, Jewish, or Egyptian?

It is impossible to ignore the fact that alchemy has, at various points in history, operated as a mystery tradition in Egypt, Greece, India, Europe, China, and the Middle East. It is because of alchemy's broad geographical spread that some have been inclined to suspect that alchemy could well be a tradition in its own right and not a mere component of other, more complete traditions. One author who investigated this branch of thought was Julius Evola, who in the preface to his work *The Hermetic Tradition* described alchemy as

> [t]he "royal" initiatory tradition, in its pure forms, [which] can be considered the most direct and legitimate link to the unique, primordial tradition [...] It is no accident that the hermetico-alchemical tradition should call itself the Royal Art, and that it chose gold as a central royal and solar symbol, which at the same time takes us back to the primordial tradition.[1]

It is clear that Evola not only believed that alchemy was a tradition in its own right, but that he also believed it had a direct link to the Primordial Tradition. However, since Hermeticism was one of Evola's favorite topics, one should take the possibility that his opinion was biased into consideration. René Guénon, in his review of *The Hermetic Tradition* in *Voile d'Isis* (published in April 1931), openly disagreed with Evola. Guénon rejected the idea that alchemy was a complete metaphysical doctrine, and instead relegated it to the ranks of a cosmological

[1] EVOLA, J., trans. REHMUS, E. E, *The Hermetic Tradition: Symbols and Teachings of the Royal Art* (Rochester, VT: Inner Traditions, 1995), xvii.

system. The basis of his rejection was that he did not believe that a genuine tradition could have migrated from an Egypto-Hellenic origin into Islamic and Christian esotericism. Guénon stated that alchemy did not function as a complete tradition in itself, but was rather always to be found integrated into other traditions, serving as an auxiliary vehicle.[2] This point of disagreement between the two authors was later repeated by Guénon in his review of Evola's edition of Cesare della Riviera's 1603 book *Il magico mondo magico de gli heroi (The Magical World of Heroes)*.

A substantial amount of the material found in alchemical texts is based on the interplay of universal symbols, which are described in the guise of laboratory practices. Even if Evola's assumption was incorrect, alchemy still managed to successfully integrate itself into all of the world's major spiritual traditions. Nonetheless, Guénon's objection remains valid, as it raises some fundamental questions. For example, why is alchemy never found as something taught on its own, but instead as an esoteric or auxiliary pathway within a larger corpus of teachings? Is it naturally to be found in symbiotic harmony with other traditions, or are there other reasons why alchemy, despite being so widespread, never became a tradition in its own right?

Given that alchemy can be found in very similar forms throughout China, India, Greece, Egypt, the Middle East, and Europe in various historical periods, it appears that the most logical explanation is also perhaps the simplest. These different branches of alchemy did not arise independently and are intimately related. The majority of scholars concur that the origins of alchemy can be found across Greek, Egyptian, and Hebrew sources. It is likewise possible that the basic symbolism underlying most forms

---

[2] Ibid., x.

of alchemy are inherited from Indo-European or Proto-Indo-European traditions, which would explain both the wide geographical dispersion of alchemy and the conformity in its cosmological structure across various systems.

The earliest writer who is known to have used the term alchemy in the West was a fourth-century astrologer, Julius Firmicus Maternus, who referenced alchemy in the following context:

> It is the House of Mercury, it gives Astronomy. That of Venus announces Songs and Joy. That of Mars, Arms [...] That of Jupiter, the Divine Cult and the Knowledge of Laws. That of Saturn, the Science of Alchemy.[3]

It is worth noting here that even at this stage, alchemy is associated with the sphere of Saturn, the planet most often linked to lead. The transformation of lead via a series of intermediary processes into gold is frequently described in alchemical texts. In the Mysteries of Mithras, lead is linked to the first step of the ladder being ascended by an initiate. Lead represents Cronus, who is the Greek equivalent of the Roman Saturn. This theme became popularized in the Middle Ages in stories of alchemists who sought to transform 'lead into gold.' Other early pieces of alchemical literature, also dating back to the fourth century, include Greek texts, which feature figures found within the *Corpus Hermeticum*: Hermes Trismegistus, Agathodaimon, Asclepius, Ammon, and Tat.[4]

---

[3] LINDSAY, J., *The Origins of Alchemy in Greco-Roman Egypt* (London: Fredrick Muller Ltd., 1970), 60.

[4] COPENHAVER, B. P., *Hermetica* (Cambridge: Cambridge University Press, 1992), xvi.

One interesting example concerning Egyptian and Hebrew alchemy is found in *A Genuine Discourse by Sophe [Kheops] the Egyptian and by the God of the Hebrews the Lord of Powers Sabaoth:* "For there are Two Sciences and Two Wisdoms: that of the Egyptians and that of the Hebrews."[5] Though this brief sentence attempts to describe the heritage of the Royal Art, it seems likely that it is more of a compromise on the part of Sophe/Kheops to demonstrate equality between two competing schools of alchemy. This rivalry between the two alchemical traditions can be seen again in the works of Maria, a female Hebrew scholar from the same period, who issued the following warning to those who use the Royal Art:

> Do not take it in your hand. It is the Igneous Remedy. [...] Do not touch it with your hands. You are not of the race of Abraham. You are not of our race.[6]

This citation clearly states that there is a distinction between the two forms of alchemy. Kabbalistic alchemy is an integral part of the Jewish Tradition, which rightly cannot be separated from it, whereas other forms of alchemy are not as heavily integrated into their respective religions. However, another alchemist from the same period believed that the roots of alchemy predate the Hebrew accounts. Zosimos claimed that alchemy was not originally part of Judaism, and stated "that their knowledge of the sacred art was achieved through fraud and then revealed."[7] Whatever the case may be, it is clear from these citations that the two forms of alchemy were not intended for the same audience, and that there were

---

[5] COPENHAVER, B. P., *Hermetica.*, 73.

[6] Ibid.

[7] Ibid.

significant differences of opinion between them. Rather than being two complementary teachings, it seems that there was heavy competition between the schools of alchemical thought, which presents a challenge to anyone researching the origins of alchemy in the Middle East.

In 1925, the search for a Middle Eastern origin for alchemy was complicated even further. R. Eisler presented an Assyrian document concerning the "maturation of metals," which he believed to be the first recorded alchemical text. Eisler developed a hypothesis based on it proposing a Mesopotamian origin for alchemy.[8] However, the quality of the translation has been debated, causing doubt as to whether this text is in fact alchemical (in the spiritual sense), since it may be a purely metallurgical text. The founder of Arabic alchemy is usually considered to be the eighth-century author Jabir ibn Hayyan, although there are records of alchemical texts in Islamic lands dating to the seventh century.[9] The Mayousaioi of Asia Minor, who combined Mazdean doctrines with Chaldean astrology, also taught something similar to alchemy, stating that the world is divided into seven millennia, each under a planet and bearing the name of an associated metal.[10] This is strikingly similar to the seven rungs on the ladder found in the mysteries of Mithras – seven of course representing the seven principal astronomical bodies, culminating in the Sun.

Alchemy is mentioned even earlier than this in Chinese records. The earliest mention of alchemy is cited

---

[8] ELIADE, M., trans. CORRIN, S., *The Forge and the Crucible: The Origins and Structure of Alchemy* (New York: Harper Torchbooks, 1971), 71.

[9] COPENHAVER, B. P., *Hemetica,* xlvi.

[10] LINDSAY, J., *The Origins of Alchemy in Greco-Roman Egypt,* 26.

in the *Huai-nan Tzu*, a text that has been dated to c. 122 BC.[11] The dating of this text indicates that alchemy was present in the Far East long before the earliest-known records of alchemical texts in the Greco-Roman/Egyptian period. Alchemy progressed along very similar lines in China and was expounded by the likes of the famous eight-century AD alchemist Lü Tsu and the magician Li Chao Kuin, who served as an alchemical advisor to Emperor Wu Ti of the Han dynasty.[12] In Tibet, the Siddha Nāgārjuna is also referred to as an alchemist. It was said by Tarānātha that through the "art of alchemy he (Nāgārjuna) maintained for many years, five hundred teachers of the Mahāyāna doctrine at Śri Nalendra."[13] Alchemical thought is predominant in Taoism as well, which, like Tantrism, maps the cosmos/metals onto the human body. In one Taoist text, cinnabar is produced by reversing the flow of sperm:

> The Taoist, imitating animals and vegetables, hangs himself upside down, causing the essence of his sperm to flow up to his brain. The *tan-t'ien*, the 'famous fields of cinnabar,' are to be found in the most secret recesses of the brain and belly: there it is that the embryo of immortality is alchemically prepared.[14]

The principal representative of Taoist-Zen alchemy, Ko Ch'ang Keng (also known as Po Yu Chaun), describes the three main forms of alchemy in the usual manner, ascribing lead to the body and mercury to the heart, as

---

[11] ELIADE, M., *The Forge and The Crucible*, 51.

[12] Ibid., quoting *Ssŭ-ma Chien*, Vol. II, pp. 465, 113.

[13] WHITE, D. G., *The Alchemical Body: Siddha Traditions In Medieval India* (Chicago: University of Chicago Press, 1996), 76.

[14] Ibid., 117.

well as '*dhyana*,' which is the medium that produces fire. Like the Western alchemists of the Middle Ages, he mentions the gestation period of forty weeks, alluding to the period during which a baby becomes fully formed in the womb. This has led some esoteric authors to assert that there are sexual elements in alchemy. It is prudent to remember that these texts were meant only for the initiated, and that their meaning is intentionally obscured for non-initiates. It thus seems improbable that the great secret of alchemy is merely sex, given that most ordinary people engage in sexual activity on a regular basis without procuring any form of spiritual or educational knowledge from it. Instead, as was the case in the Taoist text, alchemy often refers to a metaphysical operation within the body of the (usually) male practitioner concerning the 'distillation' of sperm into a '*soma*'-like substance. The sexual drive, rather than being indulged, is alchemically sublimated, and taken in a different direction than that of biological procreation. This is also what occurs in Indian alchemy.

India is sometimes mentioned as a potential source of alchemical knowledge during the same era as the Greco-Roman-Egyptian texts. Ostares, for example, states that he found three alchemical inscriptions concerning the source of alchemical knowledge: one in Egyptian, the second in Persian, and the third in Sanskrit.[15] Democritus, one of the most famous alchemists, was also reported by Doidoros to have traveled widely and left his native Ionian colony of Abdera to go to India.[16] If India had not developed alchemy before the Greeks and the Egyptians, this visit from Democritus suggests that he could have transmitted the teachings to India himself. Given these two accounts attesting to communication between India

---

[15] LINDSAY, J., *The Origins of Alchemy in Greco-Roman Egypt*, 150.

[16] Ibid., 93.

and Greece regarding alchemical matters, it explains some of the similarities between their respective traditions. It is, therefore, possible that there was also a similar transmission of teachings between China and India.

The majority of alchemical texts in India are found within the Tantric school and are very similar in content to the teachings transmitted by the Chinese, Greeks, and Egyptians. One of the essential sources for this is the *Rasārṇava*, or *Ocean of Mercury,* which is concerned with *rasavidyā* (the mercurial science). Its author makes a distinction between this branch of Tantrism and those who incorporate sexual practices into the alchemical process, stating that

> [i]f liberation came from utilizing one's semen, wine, and excrements, which of the races of dogs and swine would not be liberated? (*Ocean of Mercury*, 11-13)[17]

The author implies here that the sexually transgressive aspects to be found in some schools of Tantrism are inferior to his own, more intellectual approach. Having distanced himself from them, he then proceeds to elaborate on the wonders that arise from the study of the mercurial science:

> When swooning, mercury, like the breath, carries off diseases; when killed, it raises from the dead; when bound, it affords the power of flight. (*Ocean of Mercury*, 19)[18]

The references to the 'swooning' and 'killing' of mercury refer to alchemical processes. These practices are

---

[17] WHITE, D. G., "Ocean of Mercury" in *Tantra in Practice*, ed. WHITE, D. G. (Princeton, NJ: Princeton University Press, 2000), 284.

[18] Ibid.

comparable to the 'mortification' and 'nigredo' found in Western alchemical texts. It is also stated in the *Survarna Tantra* that by consuming 'killed mercury' (*nasta-pista*), man becomes immortal; a small quantity of this 'killed mercury' can also change lead to gold and a quantity of mercury 100,000 times as large.[19] Furthermore, in the *Kubijka Tantra*, "Shiva speaks of mercury as his generating principle and lauds its efficiency when it has been 'fixed' (i.e., killed) six times."[20] Similar terminology can found in alchemical works from the Occident.

Mercury also features strongly in other Tantric texts which are associated with the god Shiva. The *Rudrayamālā Tantra* refers to Shiva as the God of Mercury.[21] The Greeks similarly stressed the importance of mercury in their teachings: "its early Greek name, *hyrdargyros*, meant silverwater; the Latin term, *argentums vivum*, meant living silver."[22]

It is thus clear that alchemy was prevalent in many different cultures and religions across the ancient world. There are two plausible explanations for this. The first is that alchemy, as Evola says, is a tradition in its own right. The second prospect, however, is that the alchemical teachings were transmitted to all of the other locales from a single, original source. Some of the alchemical symbolism is already present in the Vedas, for example, predating all the other sources. It is therefore possible that alchemy was disseminated from India to all the other traditions as a result of Indo-European migration patterns.

---

[19]   ELIADE, M., *The Forge and the Crucible: The Origins and Structure of Alchemy*, 133.

[20]   Ibid.

[21]   Ibid.

[22]   LINDSAY, J., *The Origins of Alchemy in Greco-Roman Egypt*, 29.

The first possible reference to alchemy in the Vedic era is to be found in the *Atharva Veda* (11.3.1-2, 7,8), where metals are described as part of a cosmogonic model:

> Bṛhaspati is the head, Brahman the mouth, heaven, and earth the ears,
> Sun and moon the eyes, the Seven Seers the in-and-out-breath […]
> Dark metal its flesh, red metal its blood, tin its ash, gold its complexion.[23]

The concept of the 'body' of the cosmos being composed of minerals is also repeated in the *Śatapatha Brāmaṇa* (6.1.3. 1-5):

> Verily, Prajāpati alone was here in the beginning. He desired, "May I exist, may I reproduce myself!" He toiled, he heated himself with an inner heat. From his exhausted and overheated body the waters flowed forth…from those heated waters foam arose; from the heated foam there arose clay; from the heated clay there arose sand; from the heated sand, grit; from the heated grit, rock; from the heated rock, metallic ore; and from the smelted ore, gold arose.[24]

This passage alludes to the fact that the refinement process which transforms the foam to gold is produced utilizing an 'inner heat,' which is a reference to the process of *tapas*, an element of yogic teaching. There is also a connection between *tapas* and alchemy, as references to an 'inner fire' are also found in Western alchemy. Antoine-Joseph Pernety, for example, says that, "The Opus is accomplished

---

[23] WHITE, D. G., *The Alchemical Body: Siddha Traditions In Medieval India* (Chicago: University of Chicago Press, 1996), 12.

[24] Ibid.

neither by (vulgar) Fire nor by the hands but only by means of the inner heat."[25] The inner heat (*tapas*) is produced by controlling the breath, which is similar to the role of the Greek *pnuema* (breath). In Tantric texts, the word *hamsa* is sometimes used to symbolize the movement of energy and the *prāṇa* (vital breath), which is identical to the *pneuma*. The *Rig Veda* calls "ether (*Kha*) the 'seat' of the *hamsa*, and a series of later sources, continuing down to the Tantras, identifies inbreathing and outbreathing with the syllables *haṃ* and *saḥ*."[26]

The staff of Hermes, the caduceus, is also imbued with alchemical symbolism. The god Hermes has an obvious role to play due to his Roman name, Mercury, and also due to the fact that he is the god after which Hermeticism is named. Additionally, however, the caduceus is a potent alchemical symbol, as is verified by Epiketos the Stoic: "The power of the staff of Hermes lies in the fact that it changes all that it touched into gold."[27]

With its body embraced by twining serpents, and crowned by the wings of a bird, the caduceus is a lucrative source of spiritual symbolism. For example, the battle between Garuda and the serpentine descendants of Kadru represents a conflict between Chthonic power and Uranic power. These symbols are found together in symbiotic harmony, however, as with the caduceus, for it symbolizes mastery of both Uranic and Chthonic forces. Guénon, despite his rejection of alchemy as an independent tradition, comments on the caduceus in *The Great Triad*, and also draws a parallel to the *nāḍī* (yogic channels):

---

[25] EVOLA, J., *The Hermetic Tradition*, 142.

[26] WHITE, D. G., *The Alchemical Body*, 215.

[27] LINDSAY, J., *The Origins of Alchemy in Greco-Roman Egypt*, 33.

This is related to the general symbolism of the serpent in its two mutually opposing aspects and viewed from this angle, the double spiral itself can also be regarded as portraying a serpent coiled around itself in two opposite directions. The serpent in question will, therefore, be an '*amphis baera*' – its two hands corresponding to the two poles, and equivalent to itself to the two opposing serpents of the caduceus combined.[28]

[…]

The most notable example is the portrayal of the forces by two helicoidal lines coiling in opposite directions around a vertical axis [...] Within the human being, these two lines are the two *nādīs* or subtle currents – right and left, positive and negative (*iḍā* and *piṅgala*).[29]

By referring to these channels with their Indian names – *iḍā* and *piṅgala* – Guénon associates the caduceus with Tantrism. In Tantra there are three channels in which *kuṇḍalinī* (the Serpent Power) can ascend: the *iḍā*, *piṅgala*, and *suṣumṇā* (the central channel). In the case of the caduceus, the *iḍā* and the *piṅgala* are symbolized by the serpents, and the shaft of the staff is the *suṣumṇā*. *Kuṇḍalinī* is raised through the *cakra* until it reaches the crown cakra (*sahasrāra*), which *kuṇḍalinī* is said to 'penetrate.' *Sahasrāra* is located at the suture on the crown, where the two parietal bones meet. A similar depiction of this can also be found in the tomb of Ramses VI in Egypt, where a figure is portrayed holding a staff topped with two horns, and twin snakes. The horns which top

---

[28] GUÉNON, R., *The Great Triad* (Cambridge: St. Edmundsbury Press, 1991), 38.

[29] Ibid.

the staff are called *wpt*, which means "summit of the skull, to open, divide, separate," symbolizing the parietal bones which were believed to open and release the reborn dead.[30] Further correlations can also be seen in the *imakh:*

> Imakh (Blessed) in its ending and especially in its determinative is represented by the spinal column with an indication of the medulla; the ending also denotes the canal or channel of the spine of the snake through which the Sun passes [...] So the one symbol brings together the ideas of Blessedness, Spine, Spinal Canal (of the Sun).[31]

In these examples, there are definitely correspondences between Tantra, Hermeticism, and Egyptian alchemy which cannot be entirely coincidental. There are other correlations beyond these. The symbolism of the serpent is also found in alchemy, and the lowest metal in the alchemical hierarchy is lead, often referred to as *nāga*, "'serpent', or *sīsa[ka]*, an allomorph of the name of the cosmic serpent Śeṣa, or more rarely, Ahirāja, 'Serpent King.'"[32] In the sixteenth-century text *Rasakāmadhenu,* gold is identified as the apex of the alchemical system, and lead is traced back to Vāsuki (the king of a mythic race of serpents, from whose semen lead was first obtained).[33]

Given the number of similarities, it is easy to understand why authors such as Julius Evola view alchemy as an independent tradition. However, it is also possible to defend Rene Guénon's belief that alchemy is an esoteric auxiliary system, since in all of the cases that

[30] LINDSAY, J., *The Origins of Alchemy in Greco-Roman Egypt*, 191.

[31] Ibid.

[32] WHITE, D. G, *The Alchemical Body*, 215.

[33] Ibid.

are known, alchemy developed within the context of separate spiritual traditions, and no strictly alchemical tradition existing independently of a religion is known to exist. Thus, to a certain extent, both authors are correct in their argument. The symbolism of alchemy is universal and primordial because it is based on an understanding of the physical world and natural phenomena. Birds fly, and humans do not, so they represent the Uranic domain above, and the snake, as the closest animal to the earth, is a natural choice for a Chthonic symbol. Metals are bound by the physical laws of science, so their appearance does not change between one culture and the next. As chemistry was discovered, it would have appeared wonderous to our ancestors, and it is only natural that many of these new scientific discoveries inspired new vessels for spiritual traditions. Chemistry's miraculous revelations were translated into spiritual terms. Religions and esoteric currents sought to incorporate the new discoveries of science into the existing religions, thus making alchemical traditions neither entirely dependent on existing spiritual traditions, nor entirely separate from the original tradition. Alchemical traditions are, therefore, innovations and new developments which were built on top of an existing corpus of teachings, operating in a symbiotic relationship between mysticism and science.

DIVINING THE WILL OF THE GODS

The Ancient Science of Omens

An omen makes it possible to tell what will be one's lot – loss or gain; joy, sorrow, or unalloyed misfortune; long life or death; and the realization of one's wishes and endeavors. When two armies are locked in battle, it can tell which will win the undisputed victory, which will deal the crushing blow. In answer to the question "*What is happening in the world?*" a mortal may place his trust in the omen creatures.[1]

The Science of Omens is also referred to as the mantic tradition. Principally concerned with omens, portents, and oracles, its ritual specialists were the seers and diviners of the ancient world. The belief that omens and portents foretell the future through natural phenomena has its roots deep in the archaic past. It still survives today in practices ranging from commonly-known forms of divination such as astrology and palmistry, through to the reading of tea leaves. Omens, however, tend to utilize naturally occurring phenomena,

---

[1] WHITE, D. G., "Predicting the Future with Dogs" in *Religions of India in Practice* (Princeton, NJ: Princeton University Press, 1995), 294.

such as the behavior of animals and the weather, rather than using tools such as tarot cards or runes. This form of divination is also known as augury. It is not so common today, though a substantial amount of its legacy persists in customs and folklore. Augury is specifically concerned with the study of omens and portents in nature, which are believed to contain signals from the gods concerning forthcoming events. Augury, however, should not be confused with superstition, which is a 'folk saying' that does not involve ritual specialists. Divination via omens and portents is an *active* process, in which signals from the gods are deliberately sought – a superstition is *passive* and occurs with no active intent on the part of humans. The study of omens was once regarded as a science, and its practitioners commanded great prestige and power, enabling them to dominate the world.

The Science of Omens is the title of a chapter in a fourteenth-century text from India – the *Śārṅgadhara Padhati* (*Śārṅgadhara's Guidebook*).[2] This is a well-known work on divination and esoteric lore, and this particular chapter contains many of the usual forms of augury, such as observing the patterns of birds to predict the future, as well as other common animals. There is also material on other forms of divination, such as the throwing of dice, palmistry, astrology, and oneiromancy (the interpretation of dreams). One distinctive feature, however, is that it also describes the animal most suitable for augury and reading omens as the dog. The common canine may not appear to be a source of mystic knowledge, but in Hinduism, the dog holds a special status that is unique. The dog is what is a 'liminal' or 'threshold' animal. It is partly domesticated, but also still partially wild, like its cousin

---

[2] WHITE, D. G., "Predicting the Future with Dogs" in *Religions of India in Practice*, 288.

the wolf. The dog, therefore, sits on the boundary of man's world and the world of nature. A dog's behavior is similar to our own, and, because of this, it is easier to interpret. However, the dog's link to the world of nature still exists. As such, the dog is more receptive to communication with preternatural forces. This is why dogs are chosen for divination. They are also friendlier to humans than other animals, as is pointed out in the following extract:

> Śārṅgadhara almost immediately singles out the dog as the most eminent of all omen creatures. He clearly states his reasons for the choice: the dog's wide variety of behavior patterns, as well as its bark, is easy to understand. Dogs are, moreover, easy to come by, and easier to approach and observe than are wild animals or birds.[3]

The divination ritual is detailed in terms of structure and interpretation. It is preceded by offerings and prayers to the gods. During the ritual, the dog is granted divine status, so the dog can be used as a medium to communicate directly with the numinous. During the ritual, the dog is on a *maṇḍala* which operates as a symbolic representation of the cosmos.

> The dog is placed in the middle of a ritual diagram, on a symbolic altar upon which it is itself worshipped like a god, with flowers, incense, and so on – but upon which it is also symbolically sacrificed in the form of the baked flour-cake shaped like a brace of dogs (two dogs, like the *Sārameyau*: verses 22-23) [...] and – more importantly for the omen-master who is performing this ritual – lives to communicate future events, that is, what it has "seen" while passing beyond

---

[3]   Ibid., 289.

this world, through the world of the dead, and thereby into the future – to people trapped in the present. Oracular rituals of this sort continue to be performed, albeit in simplified form, in modern-day India, using rams and mares.[4]

Following the ritual and offerings to the gods, the reading of omens commences. The instructions for interpretation are complex and are translated into predictions of the future by reading the dog's actions at various points within the *maṇḍala*. This includes such factors as the "dog's orientation (the direction in which it is facing), movement (the movements and gestures it makes with its legs, mouth, etc.), location (the place in which it is found), motion (the direction in which it displaces itself), utterances (barking, howling, crying, etc.)."[5]

Another obscure divination technique from India involves oneiromancy, which uses dreams to predict the future. This can be found as a preliminary stage before the practice of the Six Acts. The Six Acts are outlined in the *Mantramahodadhi* and other esoteric works dealing with magico-religious practices. This extract from the *Mantramahodadhi* illustrates a ritual application of oneiromancy:

[The practitioner] who wishes to perform the worship of a deity should first consider the future. Having taken a bath, performed the twilight [ritual], and so on, [and] having collected the lotus-like feet of Hari, he should lie down on a bed of Kuśa [grass and] pray to the bull-bannered Śiva.

---

[4] WHITE, D. G., "Predicting the Future with Dogs" in *Religions of India in Practice*, 291.

[5] Ibid., 292.

"O Lord, Lord of the God of Gods, bearer of the Trident, who rides a bull! Announce, O Eternal One, the good and the bad, while I am asleep. Salutation to the Unborn, Three-eyed, Tawny, Great Souled One. Salutation to the handsome, omnipresent Lord of Dreams. Tell me the truth in the dream regarding all matters completely. O Great Lord, by Your grace I will accomplish success in the ritual."

Having prayed to Śiva with these mantras, he should sleep calmly. In the morning, he should tell the preceptor the dream he had at night. The connoisseur of the mantra should himself reflect on the [significance] of the dream [without the preceptor if he is unavailable].[6]

The text then continues to reveal a list of auspicious (good) and inauspicious (bad) omens. To receive a dream containing an auspicious omen is an indication that if the ritual is performed, it will be a success. The revelation of an inauspicious omen in the dream is indicative of the opposite; it means that Śiva has denied the rite's success, and if it is performed, the practitioner will be cursed and will accrue negative *karma*. Given the nature of the Six Acts, it is necessary to place this limitation upon the practice to prevent misuse. The role of the guru is also important for offering advice on how to interpret the omens and portents of the dreamer.

The Hellenic world and Mesopotamia also held divination in high regard, and it is from these regions that the majority of records on the study of omens and portents originate. The mantic tradition once held great power within the Mediterranean and the Middle East,

---

[6] BÜHNEMAN, G., "Six Rites of Magic" in *Tantra in Practice* (Princeton, NJ: Princeton University Press, 2000), 461.

with soothsayers and seers found within the courts of every kingdom. Texts and inscriptions, such as the *Enuma Anu-Enlil* series, are dated to the third millennium BC.[7] In the Sumerian version of the flood story Ziusudra, or Ut-Napishtim, the Babylonian Noah, is portrayed as using divinatory practices, and one of the kings, Enmeduranki of Sippur, was alleged to have obtained from the gods the art of divination.[8] From here, the science of omens in the ancient Middle East diversified; the Akkadian *barû* (a seer) studied oracles, dreams, and visions. They also read omens in the movement of water (hydromancy), the behavior of oil (lecanomancy), celestial phenomena, and the actions of animals. The barû also began to practice what could be seen today as a peculiar and barbaric technique: divination by reading the liver of a sacrificial animal (hepatoscopy). This form of divination is particularly difficult for us to comprehend in the modern era, yet to the ancient barû there was a justification for this form of augury. The liver and entrails of the animal were believed to be the core of the animal's soul, and by reading the interior marks and blemishes on the sacrificial animals 'soul,' the barû received insights into future events. Also, in Stoic theory, the internal organs represented a microcosm of the universe itself, and according to this hypothesis, a detailed examination of the liver (which was believed to be the most important bodily organ at the time) could reveal the future. The practice of hepatoscopy spread from the Middle East through to the Etruscan diviners known as haruspices, and from there expanded into the Greco-Roman world.[9]

---

[7] JAMES, E. O., *The Ancient Gods: The History and Diffusion of Religion in the Ancient Near East and the Eastern Mediterranean* (London: Readers Union Ltd., 1962), 232.

[8] Ibid., 232.

[9] Ibid., 233.

Another form of divination which is found in the Mediterranean traditions is a form of oneiromancy called dream incubation. In dream incubation, a ritual sleep is deliberately induced by the practitioner and enables the dreamer to serve as an oracle.[10] The Greek term for this was *enkamēxis*: sleeping in a sanctuary.[11] The Latin definition of incubation also implies the act of lying down and gestating in a dark, enclosed space.[12] This type of oneiromancy is also known as the *message dream*, in which a dream is experienced during the night after due preparation in the god's sanctuary.[13] This form of dream frequently appears in texts of the ancient Near East as a substitute for dream incubation.

By stressing the importance of the location in which the dream is experienced, the message dream is closely linked to the incubation dream, as the choice of location was likewise paramount. The locations in which dream incubation takes place are so closely identified with their respective gods that they were believed to be physically inhabited by the god's actual presence. Therefore, incubated dreams were referred to as god-sent (*theopemti*).[14]

---

[10] PATTERN, K. C., "'A Great and Strange Correction': Intentionality, Locality, and Epiphany in the Category of Dream Incubation" in *History of Religions,* Vol. 43, No. 3 (Chicago: University of Chicago Press, 2004), 197.

[11] Ibid., 201.

[12] Ibid., 196.

[13] BREMMER, J., *The Early Greek Concept of the Soul* (Princeton, NJ: Princeton University Press, 1983), 20.

[14] PATTERN, K. C., "'A Great and Strange Correction': Intentionality, Locality, and Epiphany in the Category of Dream Incubation" in *History of Religions,* Vol. 43, No. 3, 205.

For the Greeks, the method of incubation was based on the assumption that the *daimon*, which was only visible in the higher state achieved by the soul in dreams, had his permanent dwelling at the seat of his oracle.[15] The act of preparation to sleep in such a place constituted a ritual act, equivalent to any other ritual preparation or sacrifice in its contribution to the sacred. This particular form of divination was also incorporated in the healing of the sick, such as in the cult of the healer god Asklepios. One of the Epidaurian inscriptions reports an incident in which

> [a] man whose fingers were paralyzed had a dream that he was playing dice, and just when he was about to make a throw, the god suddenly appeared, jumped on his hand and stretched out his fingers, and straightened them one by one. As the day dawned, he left the temple cured, although at first, he had doubted the accounts of the cures he had read on the tablets in the precincts of the sanctuary.[16]

Although the cult of Asklepios eventually spread to Rome in the form of the Aesculapium, prior to this, divination amongst the Romans was focused on the reading of omens via the natural world, such as the flight of birds or the behavior of lightning. Lightning was assumed to reflect the direct will of Jupiter, the king of the gods who ruled over the sky.

> The place where lightning struck was immediately declared holy because it seemed that Jupiter had claimed it for himself. The area, called bidental, was enclosed, and sacrifices and prayers were made there.

---

[15] ROHDE, E., *Psyche: The Cult of Souls and Belief in Immortality Among the Greeks,* Vol. 1 (New York: Harper Torchbooks, 1996), 92.

[16] Ibid., 241.

[...] Thunder was also studied. There survives, at third hand, a calendar which gives the significance of thunder-claps on each day of the year. Thus if it thunders on 3 December, a shortage of fish will make people eat meat; if it thunders on 19 August, women and slaves will commit murder.[17]

Roman religion was focused on the belief that the divine will could be ascertained from signs and omens that occurred naturally, but in the form of extraordinary phenomena. This idea is connected to Stoicism, which held that the universe was composed of a fiery spirit that permeated everything and that "this rational spirit ordained and controlled everything which happened."[18] One of the official forms of divination in Rome came from the observance of birds.

In Rome there was a special site (the auguraculum) on the Capital which was reserved for the purpose and the magistrate would be accompanied by one of the college of fifteen augurs, distinguished figures like himself, who pronounced the ceremonial formula for designating the quarter of the sky and would interpret, blind-folded, any signs which the magistrate reported. The practice was regarded so seriously that when in 99 BC, T. Claudius Centumalus built a house which obstructed the view from the auguraculum he was forced to pull it down.[19]

The practice was not limited to wild birds, for like their Hindu counterparts, the Romans saw the benefits of

[17] R. M. OGILVIE, *The Romans and Their Gods* (London: Pimlico, 2000), 59.

[18] Ibid., 54.

[19] Ibid., 56.

keeping domesticated animals for the purposes of divination. Specially-raised chickens known as *pullarii* were used for augury by the Romans, especially when on military expeditions, as the birds could be transported easily.

Because the mantic tradition was widespread through the Middle East and the Mediterranean regions, there are numerous records of its practice, diligently preserved by Classical scholars and archeologists. When it comes to studying the science of omens in European traditions, however, the task becomes significantly more difficult due to the gradual erosion of European traditions over many hundreds of years. The reconstruction of indigenous European beliefs is a challenging task, compounded by the lack of research in this area. Whilst it is widely known that both trance work and runes were employed as divinatory techniques in pagan Europe, the ritual and religious practices of the region have not been studied in the same manner as those of Greece, Rome, and the Middle East. Because of this, there is little conclusive evidence as to how and what techniques were actually used.

Despite this, there are instances of divination via omens and portents in European traditions. For example, a Gaelic rite of divination called *taghairm* was practiced in the following manner:

> A man is wrapt in the warm skin of an animal just killed, he is then lain down beside a waterfall in the forest, and left alone; by the roar of the waves, it is thought, the future is revealed to him.[20]

---

[20]   GRIMM, J., *Teutonic Mythology*, Vol. III (New York: Dover Publications, 2004), 1115.

The Teutons had intricate systems for reading omens from the behavior of animals. However, unlike the Roman, who used domestic livestock for oracular readings, the Teutons deemed domesticated animals to be unsuitable for augury. There are also fewer instances of birds being used for divination, despite the fact that birds were thought to be the messengers of the gods in the Northern mysteries.[21] The birds that were studied for signs of omens and portents were frequently birds of prey. Ravens and crows also held a position of prominence. The Teutons had special titles for their diviners, including *heilisôn*, *heilisôd*, *heilisari*, and *heilisara*, which are all equivalents of the term augury.[22] This may have also been a hereditary position, as Jacob Grimm states:

> A female fortune-teller declared that the gift had long been in her family, and on her death would descend to her eldest daughter: from mother to daughter, therefore, and from father to son; by some, it is maintained that soothsaying and the gift of healing must be handed down from women to men, from men to women.[23]

The science of omens was at one time employed by the major civilizations of the ancient world, and its techniques were as varied as its practice was widespread. The practitioners of this ancient art were accorded with titles and rank, sometimes with power so great their prophecies and predictions shaped the destinies of empires and the fortunes of war. Though some of their techniques may seem unusual, we must ask ourselves how such practices

---

[21] Ibid., 11128.

[22] Ibid., 11106.

[23] Ibid., 11107.

could be relevant today. The study of dreams, now the subject of psychology, may not reveal the future, but it does reveal the dreamer's subconscious attitude and the implications of personal issues on the dreamer's life. As such, dreams have been proven to have a very real impact on our waking life. With our knowledge of science and advanced understanding of man's role in the natural world, humanity is now progressing towards a sense of unity with the environment. We are learning not to pillage the Earth and are attempting to restore the precocious balance between civilization and nature, reminding ourselves that we are not separate from the forces of nature. Observing the behavior of animals may not foretell the future directly, but unlike humans, animals have not lost their natural instincts, which tie them closely to the environment they inhabit. In humans, this instinct is subdued. There are few biologists who would doubt that an animal can foretell the weather or natural events better than a human, and it is precisely for this reason that our ancestors chose to rely upon the study of natural phenomena for the science of omens; what they were reading was the will of nature, which in many ways is a direct experience of the will of the gods.

MODERN RELEVANCE

PERENNIAL PHILOSOPHY IN THE CONTEMPORARY ERA

n recent years, there has been a coordinated effort from minor political organizations to appropriate the ideas of perennial philosophy, which began by co-opting the term 'Traditionalism' (referring to adherents of Traditional religions) and transforming its original meaning to a purely political one (Traditionalism as a political ideology). For the most part, political Traditionalism has been too marginal to attract any significant interest from the mainstream, but it was elevated in popularity during the brief wave of American interest in the Alt-Right during 2016-2017, which swiftly waned into total disgrace for all involved.

A cursory examination of the now spectacularly defunct Alt-Right reveals two issues. Firstly, there was a swath of individuals who advocated a form of 'Traditional Living,' which was devoid of any genuine religious sentiment, philosophy, or higher purpose. The second problem were those peddling deliberately falsified spiritual or philosophical ideas, along with 'fake history,' all designed to support infeasible political agendas. This poorly-organized conglomerate of ostracized individuals peaked during Donald Trump's first campaign, through the Alt-Right's manipulation of social media algorithms (referred to as 'meme magick,' or more correctly, continuously spamming internet users with pro-Trump propaganda).

There was one plot twist, however, related to perennial philosophy. The *AltRight.com* website, which presented itself as the official portal for the 'movement,' republished an article entitled 'Against Perennial Philosophy' that had previously appeared on the *RightOn.net* site. This article argued that all perennial philosophy was based on Islamic sources, and should, therefore, be disregarded. This only succeeded in widening the existing schism between perennial philosophy and Traditionalism, eventually culminating in the final doom-spiral of the Alt-Right itself. The terms Traditionalist and Traditionalism should be avoided to prevent confusion with any lingering political movements still using the terms. However, pruning the dross from one's garden still has to amount to more than removing a few unpleasant weeds. It also requires the cultivation of healthy ideas to grow, blossom, and eventually bear fruit in their stead. One must counter a negative ideology with a positive one. Perennial philosophy should therefore not just counter the dead weight *against* it; it has to supplant political Traditionalism entirely, and stand *for* something.

Ideally, a new definition of cultural identity is required to circumnavigate the excessively hyperpartisan mentality endemic to the United States, which ultimately had more to do with the creation of the Alt-Right than its founders did. Moreover, it must be replaced by a fully meritocratic platform, based on actual achievements and demonstrated abilities, rather than mere privileges of birth allocated by superficial physical attributes. Only then can a new, vibrant culture flourish. This issue is one of paramount importance for a civilization to function as a whole. True perennial philosophy can assist here by redefining the interpretation of cultural identity itself. Furthermore, this transmission must be cultural, never political.

Though the *Sophia Perennis* is a fixed universal truth, the same cannot be said of human interpretations of spiritual traditions, particularly when they are appropriated for political pursuits and propaganda. These deliberately embellished adaptations are designed to proselytize the masses with fictitious rhetoric, trading under the label of 'politics.' In the current era, this behavior is so prolific that it is now commonplace, and people who would never have been permitted to represent a tradition pretend to be authorities, which is detrimental to the entire public perception of religion and spirituality. This, however, is characteristic of the nature of the Age itself – *dharma* and spiritual law only operates at full strength in a Golden Age or Satya Yuga. Over the cycle of ages, it weakens, and in the last age – the Iron Age, Kali Yuga, or Wolf Age – traditional law wavers, and eventually is eroded entirely before a new Golden Age of prosperity commences.

For spiritual traditions to survive and adapt to contemporary society, they must reach an audience that is unreceptive to new ideas and critical of past ones. A new transmission is required that is capable of reinterpreting the language of the *Sophia Perennis* and conveying its language in a medium and mode appropriate to the current era. Perennial philosophy itself does not change, but the medium through which it communicates does – and that which does not adapt is doomed to perish.

In the previous chapters, the substitution of the term Primordial Tradition for perennial philosophy was mentioned, and this can also be extended into the cultural realm. The Primordial Tradition is rightly defined as being

a *sui generis* argument, meaning that it is self-generating
– a concept which originated with Émile Durkheim.
Sui generis is a Latin expression, literally meaning "of
its own kind/genus," or unique in its characteristics. In
this circumstance, religion is deemed to be composed
of archetypal concepts that are inherent in the psyche
from the dawn of consciousness itself. Like society,
they are naturally occurring. This implies a relationship
with Jungian thought and links it to Jung's theory of the
subconscious and archetypes as symbols which, whilst
they are not possessed of corporeal existence, act as
what he called 'psychoids.' The language of tradition is,
therefore, symbolist in origin. Symbols and patterns of
belief shape the cultures of the world around them. When
minor discrepancies can be found among the archetypes
if examined through cross-cultural comparison, they are
easily explained as being a different translation of the same
archetype or symbol in a specific cultural context, for it
is imperative to remember that not all cultural groups in
the world share the same set of psychological processes;
each culture has been shaped by different historical,
geographical, natural, and social forces. Thus the God of
an indigenous shamanic population may appear radically
different to the God of the Jews or Christians, though
all are speaking of the same entity. The foundational
premise of the symbol is the same as that of an archetypal
phenomenon. However, the translation itself is parsed
through each environment differently.

A *sui generis* argument is classified as self-perpetuating
because it originates from a concept that is deemed to exist
from the beginning. In Durkheim's sociology, a *sui generis*
argument is used to illustrate his theory on social existence.
Durkheim states that the main object of sociology is to
study social facts. These social facts can only be explained

by other social phenomena. They have a meaning of their own and cannot be reduced to psychological or biological factors. Social facts have a meaning of their own. They are a '*sui generis*.' Durkheim also states that when one takes an organization and replaces some individuals with others, the essence of the organization does not (necessarily) change. It can happen, for example, that over the course of a few decades, the entire staff of an organization is replaced, while the organization itself still retains its distinctive character. Durkheim does not limit this idea to organizations, but rather extends it to the whole of society: he maintains that society, as it was there before any particular living individual was born, is independent of all individuals. This *sui generis* (its closest English meaning in this sense being 'independent') society will furthermore continue its existence after the individual ceases to interact with it. Society and culture are, therefore, organic and naturally arising phenomena.

If we are to accept spirituality as a self-generating phenomenon set apart from the world of the mundane by its inherent qualities of the sacred and transcendent, how can we relate this process to the construction of cultural identity? Both spiritual beliefs and society are self-generating and self-perpetuating without the need for any artificial intervention – in sum, both are organic, living forms of belief and awareness which are to be found in all peoples, for they are universal values. Though at first the concept of an organic model of identity may appear like a radical transition, it is, in fact, not. Nations are born from ancient, natural phenomena, and thus shape themselves when constructing an identity. This stands in radical contrast to the modern views of the inorganic, modernist view of nationality, which is developed and guided by external forces.

101

Similar notions can be found in German Romanticism, such as the works of Johann Gottlieb Fichte and Johann Gottfried Herder. Herder's theories revolved around the use of language in cultural groupings. For Herder, the concept of the nation was synonymous with its linguistic group, which he also held to be a reflection of the group's thought processes. Thus, each linguistic grouping would have not only different languages but a different thought process. This is highly indicative of linguistic groupings being one of the primary sources from which national identities are formed. Accordingly, all people who spoke the same dialect were part of the community.

Another important element that plays a key role in the assertion of cultural identities is the landscape itself. Anthony D. Smith suggests that "the landscapes of the nation define and characterize the identity of its people."[1] Land and geographical features will always be a universal element within any cultural grouping, for they generate images to which all members of the populace can relate:

> Landscape is itself a representation, 'a medium [...] embedded in a tradition of cultural signification and communication, a body of symbolic forms capable of being invoked and reshaped to express meaning and values' (Mitchell 1994: 14). The interpretation of landscapes is hence a politically loaded activity: the meaning attributed to them results from an ideologically coded interpretation of society and nation (Nogué and Vicente 2004). Landscapes function in nation-building discourses as symbols of national authenticity. For this purpose, nature

---

[1]   BAIRNER, A., "National Sports and National Landscapes" in *National Identities*, Vol. 11, No. 3 (Milton Park, Oxfordshire: Taylor & Francis, September 2009), 224.

can be nationalized, but by associating nationhood with a landscape the nation can itself be naturalized (Kaufmann and Zimmer 1998; Smith 1986: 183–90).[2]

The notion of sacred land is also found in almost all indigenous cultures, particularly in locations where natural phenomena were unusual; thus, not only did land shape the evolution of society, it is also intrinsically wed to spirituality. These sites often become associated with myth, pilgrimage, and ritual. Furthermore, the appeal of the landscape in defining cultural identity is not limited to inhabitants of localized regions; it is also significantly embodied in constructing the identity of diasporic groups. In this respect, the fact that nations are defined territorially (although in relation to diasporic nationals, they can also transcend spatial boundaries) is an essential factor in their emotional appeal, especially when one considers the importance of the landscape for any territorial entity.[3] A prominent example of the use of the landscape as a construct of national identity amongst diasporic peoples would be the establishment of Israel as the homeland of the Jews.

Many indigenous peoples also understand the importance of scared land. It is logical to assume that any group of people cohabiting a particular geographic region for a period of time would form the necessary social bonds which would act as a precursor to the formation of a rudimentary community, and that this community would in turn associate the land upon which they lived as part of their national identity. This, however, is only a small portion of the issue.

---

[2] HUYSSEUNE, M., "Landscapes as a Symbol of Nationhood" in *Nations and Nationalism,* No. 16, Vol. 2 (2010), 355.

[3] BAIRNER, A., "National Sports and National Landscapes," 225.

Clifford Geertz is usually credited as the author who introduced the concept of the primordial attachments and sentiments of an individual to the world.[4] In Geertz's theory, these factors are the assumed normative functions present in human social groupings. According to Geertz, one is bound to one's kinsman, one's neighbor, and one's fellow believer – *ipso facto* not only as the result of personal affection, practical necessity, common interest, or obligation, but by the importance attributed to the very tie itself.[5] The nature of the attachments themselves are not constants and vary between individuals and communities. In a modern democracy, these factors occur in combination, which ensures that the normal social bonding processes take place within the community: language, culture, and group psychology all occur within the formative process. This is similar to Victor Turner's theory of *communitas*.

Victor Turner is a prominent figure in the field of anthropology. The idea of *communitas* put forward by Turner revolves around an interplay of spiritual traditions in order to form bonds within social groupings. This intangible bond by which people identify their sense of 'belonging' is what Turner refers to as *communitas*. In terms of relevance for cultural identity, it is vital to understand what creates the sentiments that form these attachments in the collective psychology of the nation. A political scientist, Walter Connor, once analyzed the speeches of the great leaders of nations, as well as national revivalists, and noted that a conspicuous uniformity of phraseology was observable in a number of these speeches:

---

[4] BAÈOVÁ, V., "The Construction of National Identity" in *Human Affairs*, No. 8 (Institute of Social Sciences, Slovak Academy of Sciences, 1998), 4.

[5] Ibid., 31.

Phrases and pictures of family, blood, brothers, sisters, mothers, ancestors, home were almost universal. The speeches and phrases were able to mobilize masses, and many individuals also believed them in private. W. Connor justifies the force of these appeals to primordial attachments by their emotional strength through which they have affected and continue to affect the human mind.[6]

Connor's analysis paints a very clear picture of the political uses of not only cultural attachments but also the effects of successfully raising the *vital impetus* in respective audiences. A quick examination of speeches by the former President of the United States, George W. Bush, reveals a highly targeted usage of keywords and phrases such as 'freedom' and the 'axis of evil.' Though Bush's use of emotion in politics pales in comparison to others, attempts to evoke sentimental responses in his political speeches are present, and this is demonstrated by an excessive repetition of phrases and carefully selected words that were targeted to rouse the American public. More recently, Donald Trump has opted for a tactic that preferences direct emotional manipulation instead of a cohesive strategy, which is evident in his reliance on rallies and social media for the cultivation of political sentiment, as opposed to the logical implementation of policy and procedure. However, these elements were also present in Far Left ideologies. For example, Mao's speeches suggest that the use of emotive language was not limited to any Left- or Right-wing ideology. Indeed, as a universal element in the cultural spheres, the use of an 'appeal to emotion' is prevalent across the entire political spectrum.

---

[6] Ibid., 41.

Emotion is a driving force in the construction of cultural identities and has been utilized for both good and bad agendas. In a smaller community, where communal bonds are more robust, theorists struggle to explain how these bonds give rise to culture. This is not a great mystery. There is merely a need to generate more profound emotional responses to enhance the existing feelings of *communitas* to a point where they are replicated in the creations of the people themselves, for aesthetics represents the 'soul of the nation' just as a spiritual tradition is the spirit of the people. Baèová paraphrases this, albeit in the context of nationalism, stating that "[a] ccording to some authors, the success of nationalism can today be explained by the fact that it made an efficient use of the strength of human primordial attachments and extended them to a macrocommunity, i.e., to the nation-state."[7]

Steve Bruce argues that religion (or a spiritual tradition) is greatly underestimated as a force in contemporary Western society, both in terms of literal belief and in terms of its symbolic and metaphorical meaning.[8] Furthermore, as structural-functionalism has declined in the social sciences as a theoretical tool of analysis, so too have the functional aspects, and the relevance of spiritual traditions has been overlooked.[9] Indeed, in the Occident, spiritual traditions are often misunderstood; for every step forward taken with scientific progress, research in the humanities has taken

---

[7] Ibid., 38.

[8] DINGLEYA, J., "Religion, Truth, National Identity, and Social Meaning: The Example of Northern Ireland" in *National Identities*, Vol. 11, No. 4 (Milton Park, Oxfordshire: Taylor & Francis, December 2009), 367.

[9] Ibid., 368.

about twenty steps backward. The destruction of culture, the province of the humanities, will eventually erode the foundation of the modern nation-state, as it is only the shared experience of cultural identity that binds the entire population together. The impact of different spiritual traditions on identity, whether they have had positive or adverse effects, has – and continues to be – a driving force in human culture. As Durkheim concluded, "If religion has given birth to all that is essential in society, it is because the idea of society is the soul of religion." Thus, in Durkheim's view society and religion are fundamentally linked. Even a cursory glance at the etymological origins of both religion and society reveals just how deep the connection between the two is. The word 'religion' comes from the Latin *religio*, meaning bonds of social relations; 'society' comes from the Latin *socio*, meaning bonds of compassion and community.[10] The appropriate role of spirituality is, therefore, one of social relationships, which serve to define a network or community. This definition would exclude all forms of 'political religion,'[11] which instead defines an individual's role primarily in relation to the state.

> Religion thus implies the idea of networks and relations superior to the individual that perform life-enhancing, even life-creating functions. They create a sense of community and compassion because its members share relationships, thus was Durkheim able to identify God and religion as society. The

---

[10] Ibid., 369.

[11] The theory of political religion concerns governmental ideologies whose cultural and political backing is so fanatical that they attain power equivalent to that of a state religion. Political religions compete with genuine spiritual traditions, and attempt to replace or eradicate them.

relationships one enters into also help form one's consciousness and culture and thus one's identity, sense of place, and belonging. Relationships convey knowledge and information, ways of interpreting the world, and understanding one's place in it – skills vital to maintaining one's life in terms of social interaction, economic cooperation, material survival, and physical (military) preservation.[12]

Therefore, if used correctly, religion should serve to bring a community together; only when religion falls into the hands of politics does it become warped for extremist political agendas. Having demonstrated how spirituality can be distorted by political rhetoric, it behooves us to explain what the appropriate role for spiritual traditions should be in the context of cultural identities. As Rudolf Otto says "if there be any single domain of human experience that presents us with something unmistakably specific and unique, peculiar to itself, assuredly it is that of the religious life." The nature of a spiritual belief ties an individual to a community more strongly than ethnicity does, and it is more effective for shaping cultural identities. Moreover, the acceptance of the same value system equates to a similar ethical viewpoint, which in turn creates a more harmonious society. By way of contrast, geographical or ethnic attachments produce weaker social bonds, and the principle of *communitas* is lessened. A shared spiritual tradition or belief is more powerful than external appearances in terms of political and cultural factors.

Membership in a community by virtue of one's ethnic descent is not sufficient to explain the cultural groupings

[12] DINGLEYA, J., "Religion, Truth, National Identity and Social Meaning: The Example of Northern Ireland," 369.

of the modern era. Not only are there now significant communities of mixed ethnicity, but there are also the newly emerging micro-communities to consider, which although currently limited to social networking do exhibit the same patterns as newly-developing nations in the sense that the social bonds are naturally arising from communal attachments, which are usually based on culture or lifestyle. In the present era, any political theory or ideology which holds ethnicity to be the primary emotional attachment is destined to fail. Ernest Gellner, for his part, suggests that cultural identity could instead be conferred through language and education:

> According to him, nationalism means a transfer of the focus of people's identity into a culture that is disseminated through literacy and the formal system of education. It is not the mother tongue (i.e., primordial attachment) that is important anymore, but the language of *alma mater* (as an instrumental means of communication).[13]

Language acts as the primary focus for creating social bonds, and is perhaps the most crucial element in constructing cultural identity, for, without a collective linguistic group, there can be no opportunities for bonding within the community. When channeled into education via the medium of language, the culture and society prescribe the value of the nation to an individual.[14] Cultural identity, fostered by the emotional attachments, passes through the contemporary educational system, and it is in this way that culture is disseminated.

---

[13] BAÈOVÁ, V., "The Construction of National Identity," 38-39.

[14] Ibid., 43.

In conclusion, there must be a clear demarcation drawn between perennial philosophy and politicized 'Traditionalism.' The most straightforward way to achieve this is by avoiding the terms Traditionalism and Traditionalist, which now have an altogether different meaning than they did in the past. Moreover, those who are interested in perennial philosophy would do well to avoid being closely associated with any political organizations. Instead, the role of perennial philosophy and spiritual traditions is one of guru-like detachment. One is aware of such activities and all their ramifications, but one does not participate unless it is vital to do so, for the success or failure of political organizations is predetermined by external criteria long before they even utter their first statement. The true master of a spiritual tradition knows the fate of an organization from the beginning and simply waits for the river to run its course. It is not necessary to intervene, because the opposing current is always destined to fail. This, however, does not entail passivity, but rather a sage-like disposition that does not waste one's energy attacking things which are already doomed to perish, nor attempting to save that which is no longer salvageable.

Detachment in the realm of politics does not disempower perennial philosophy. On the contrary, it invigorates the role of spiritual traditions in society by separating them from temporary political fashions, which, in modern democracies, all have a minimal lifespan. Just as there were distinctions between the priests and the warriors in ancient societies, so too are their distinctions between intellectuals and politicians. The role of philosophy is contemplative and speculative. It is not legislative nor manipulative, nor should it ever attempt to become so. Instead, perennial philosophy should concentrate on the cultural and social elements of spiritual traditions. This is by no means a lesser role, as it shapes the cultural identities of the citizens of the future, and those citizens will ultimately select their political leaders – possibly those of a very different type from those on offer today.

Cultural identity is created through shared languages, history, and symbols such as the landscape and environment, which are elements that serve to unite the people in a positive and constructive fashion, in contrast to outdated models of citizenship based on physical traits which now sow division and malcontent. In terms of spiritual traditions, by studying and understanding the shared features, narrative, and symbols, humanity can realize how religions form, dissolve into each other, and eternally recur anew, as part of the Primordial Tradition. The nature of perennial philosophy, when untarnished by political misapplication, serves to reveal the commonality of the human experience – the triumphs, challenges, and woes which are universal to all humans, and which bind us together as a civilization.

ABOUT THE AUTHOR

Gwendolyn Taunton was born in Queensland (Australia) and raised in Christchurch (New Zealand). She relocated back to Australia following a series of destructive earthquakes in 2010-2011.

Gwendolyn has an extensive academic background in Philosophy, Hinduism, Buddhism, and Information Technology. In 2009 she won the $10,000 *Ashton Wylie Award for Literary Excellence* for her first book *Primordial Traditions*, which was presented by the Mayor of Auckland. She has previously been employed as a graphic designer and web developer for the University of Canterbury and the Ministry of Research, Science, & Technology.

Her natural habit is a spacious home in rural Australia, filled with books, animals, exotic plants, and religious antiquities. Gwendolyn is strongly pro-environment and is concerned with animal welfare.